A HUGE THUMBS UP FOR THE FILM CLUB

"A touching coming-of-age story for both father and son."
—*Time Out Chicago*

"A heartfelt portrait of how hard it is to grow up, how hard it is to watch someone grow up, and how in the midst of a family's confusion and ire, there is sometimes nothing so welcome as a movie . . . Like any good parent, [Gilmour] focuses on his son and he makes us care very much about what happens to him . . . he has my admiration as a father for making his son, not himself, the very winning hero of this story. Not only did I find Jesse smart and funny, but more than once I was moved to tears by his battle to find his place."
—Douglas McGrath, *New York Times Book Review*

"[A] smart memoir . . . Gilmour keeps THE FILM CLUB from lapsing into a *Tuesdays with Morrie* sugar-high through sharp writing and pointed insights about the films he screens and the people who made them."
—*Newsday*

"A winning account that should appeal to 1) former teenagers, especially guys who have loved and lost; 2) parents of teenagers or former teenagers; and 3) anyone who loves movies."
—*Chicago Tribune*

more . . .

"Funny and heartwarming . . . A charming memoir filled with moments of insight and wit."
—*Miami Herald*

"'A-' [A] page-turning account . . . Gilmour's a clear, breezy writer, and his book's got a lot of heart; ultimately, it becomes subtly affecting."
—*Entertainment Weekly*

"A great book for dads and movie lovers."
—*Newark Star-Ledger*

"[A] wry, wondrous memoir . . . so keenly observed and delightfully drawn is its story of a troubled father and a troubled son, and how cinema saves them . . . I found that I had become completely enraptured by David and Jesse."
—*Buffalo News*

"One of the delights of this book is Gilmour's smart, passionate, immensely knowledgeable writing about movies . . . But the book is also a refreshingly straightforward look at the joys and sorrows of parenting a teenage boy . . . You can't rewind your kid's childhood, and Gilmour's experience suggests that what really counts, for parent and child, is simply being together."
—*St. Petersburg Times*

"Intimate and confessional . . . challenges our notions of education, productivity, of schools that fail to inspire. It is also a tender account of a parent's deep concern for his child."
—*Toronto Globe and Mail*

"The film talk is as interesting as the parental angst . . . But in the end, this is a quiet book about being a father, loving a boy, and doing what you can to shore him up, and then, proudly but sadly, let him go."
—*Arizona Republic*

"Fascinating . . . a marvelous mashup—part middle-age memoir, part movie trivia, part glimpse into how boys uneasily morph into men."
—*Chicago Sun-Times*

"[An] unexpectedly delicate memoir . . . Gilmour is good with little observations that tell larger truths . . . Gilmour is upfront about himself, as well."
—*Palm Beach Post*, as well as the Cox newswire service

"Dynamic . . . heartwarming . . . With ironic wit and self-introspection, [Gilmour] beautifully analyzes the slow but transforming effect the films had on his son . . . Perfectly balanced recollections, brimming with pathos leavened by sardonic humor."
—*Kirkus Reviews*

more . . .

"THE FILM CLUB tells such an unusual story, and tells it so gracefully . . . I was hooked on Gilmour's spare, limpid style, and on the tenderness, bitter sweetness, and the film education that I could feel unfolding from the first page . . . THE FILM CLUB is a deep pleasure to read, almost as much fun as—or maybe more than—going to the movies."
—HuffingtonPost. com

"If all sons had dads like David Gilmour, then Oedipus would be a forgotten legend and Father's Day would be a worldwide film festival."
—Sean Wilsey, author of *Oh the Glory of It All*

"A wise and winning small book that demonstrates a lot about the power of film."
—*Charleston Post and Courier*

"Sensitive . . . Both for its smart, engaging movie talk and for its touching depiction of a father-son relationship, THE FILM CLUB gets two thumbs way up."
—*Booklist*

"David Gilmour is a very unlikely moral guidance counselor . . . Yet when it looks as though his teenage son is about to go off the rails, he reaches out to him through the only subject he knows anything about: the movies. The result is an object lesson in how fathers should talk to their sons."
—Toby Young, author of
How to Lose Friends and Alienate People

"What makes the story so readable is its mix of sentiment and cynicism, its cockeyed wisdom . . . Gilmour is a brave writer and a brave father. He is determined to discuss things with his son that most fathers would probably rather not know about. His courage is rewarded with a new, deeper understanding of his beloved child."
—*Ottawa Citizen*

"Poignant and witty . . . Expertly tracing the trials and tribulations of teenage crushes and heartbreak . . . Gilmour expertly tackles the nostalgia not only of film but also that of parents, watching as their children grow and develop separate lives. With his unique blend of film history and personal memoir, Gilmour's latest offering will deservedly win him new American fans."
—*Publishers Weekly*

more . . .

"An excellent choice for a book club, and it's as good as a David Gilmour novel. That's saying a lot."
—*Toronto Star*

"Meaningful, insightful, valuable . . . On a social level alone, it challenges our notions of education, of productivity, of high schools that have fallen catastrophically behind in their capability to inspire young men."
—Charles Wilkins, *The Globe and Mail*

"A touching and memorable tribute from a father to his son."
—*Louisville Courier Journal*

"I love Gilmour's sleek, potent little memoir. It's so, so wise in the ways of fathers and sons, of movies and moviegoers, of love and loss."
—Richard Russo, Pulitzer Prize–winning author of *Empire Falls*

"A deeply affecting parenting manual . . . a disarmingly fun way for a grown man to connect with his young son . . . the fact that he can actually lead his son into the decision he makes at the end of the book makes it a particularly special and remarkable one . . . a great memoir . . . just about anyone can benefit from its wisdom."
—BookReporter.com

"What makes the story so readable is its mix of sentiment and cynicism, its cockeyed wisdom . . . Gilmour is a brave writer and a brave father."
—Joel Yanofsky, *National Post*

The
Film
CLUB

Other Books by David Gilmour

The Film CLUB

David Gilmour

TWELVE

New York   Boston

Twelve

Hachette Book Group

237 Park Avenue

New York, NY 10017

Visit our Web site at www.HachetteBookGroup.com.

Twelve is an imprint of Grand Central Publishing.

The Twelve name and logo are trademarks of Hachette Book Group, Inc.

Printed in the United States of America

Originally published in hardcover by Twelve.

First Trade Edition: June 2009

10 9 8 7 6 5 4 3 2

The Library of Congress has cataloged the hardcover edition as follows:

Gilmour, David

  The film club / David Gilmour. — 1st ed.

    p. cm.

  Includes index.

  ISBN: 978-0-446-19929-2 (alk. paper)

  1. Gilmour, David, 1949– 2. Gilmour, Jesse. 3. Fathers and sons. 4. High school dropouts. 5. Motion pictures and teenagers. 1. Title.

  CT275.G4325A3 2008

  920—dc22

                                                                2007023395

ISBN: 978-0-446-19930-8 (pbk.)

Book design by Charles Sutherland

To Patrick Crean

I know nothing about education except this: that the greatest and most important difficulty known to human beings seems to lie in that area which deals with how to bring up children and how to educate them.

—MICHEL DE MONTAIGNE (1533–92)

CHAPTER 1

I WAS STOPPED AT A RED LIGHT the other day when I saw my son coming out of a movie theater. He was with his new girlfriend. She was holding his coat sleeve at the very end with her fingertips, whispering something into his ear. I didn't catch what film they'd just seen—the marquee was blocked by a tree in full flower—but I found myself remembering with a gust of almost painful nostalgia those three years that he and I spent, just the two of us, watching movies, talking on the porch, a magic time that a father doesn't usually get to have so late in a teenage boy's life. I don't see him now as much as I used to (that's as it should be) but that was a gorgeous time. A lucky break for both of us.

When I was a teenager, I believed that there was a place where bad boys went when they dropped out of school. It was somewhere off the edge of the earth, like that graveyard for elephants, only this one was full of the delicate white bones of little boys. I'm sure that's why, to this day, I still have nightmares about studying for a physics exam, about flipping, with escalating worry, through page after page of my textbook—vectors and parabolas—because *I've never seen any of this stuff before!*

Thirty-five years later, when my son's marks began to wobble in grade nine and toppled over entirely in grade ten, I experienced a kind of double horror, first at what was actually happening, second from this remembered sensation, still very alive in my body. I switched homes with my ex-wife ("He needs to live with a man," she said). I moved into her house, she moved into my loft, which was too small to accommodate the full-time presence of a six-foot-four, heavy-footed teenager. That way, I assumed privately, *I* could do his homework for him, instead of her.

But it didn't help. To my nightly question "Is that all your homework?" my son, Jesse, responded with a cheerful "Absolutely!" When he went to stay with his mother for a week that summer, I found a hundred different homework assignments shoved into every conceivable hiding place in his bedroom. School, in a word, was making him a liar and a slippery customer.

We sent him to a private school; some mornings, a bewildered secretary would call us. "Where is he?" Later that day, my long-limbed son would materialize on the porch. Where had he been? Maybe to a rap competition in some shopping mall in the suburbs or someplace less savory, but not school.

We'd give him hell, he'd apologize solemnly, be good for a few days, and then it would all happen again.

He was a sweet-natured boy, very proud, who seemed incapable of doing anything he wasn't interested in, no matter how much the consequences worried him. And they worried him a great deal. His report cards were dismaying except for the comments. People liked him, all sorts of people, even the police who arrested him for spray-painting the walls of his former grade school. (Incredulous neighbors recognized him.) When the officer dropped him off at the house, he said, "I'd forget about a life of crime, if I were you, Jesse. You just don't have it."

Finally, in the course of tutoring him in Latin one afternoon, I noticed that he had no notes, no textbook, nothing, just a wrinkled-up piece of paper with a few sentences about Roman consuls he was supposed to translate. I remember him sitting head down on the other side of the kitchen table, a boy with a white, untannable face in which you could see the arrival of even the smallest upset with the clarity of a slammed door. It was Sunday, the kind you hate when you're a teenager, the weekend all but over, homework undone, the city gray like the ocean on a sunless day. Damp leaves on the street, Monday looming from the mist.

After a few moments I said, "Where are your notes, Jesse?"

"I left them at school."

He was a natural at languages, understood their internal logic, had an actor's ear—this should have been a breeze—

but watching him flip back and forth through the textbook, I could see he didn't know where anything was.

I said, "I don't understand why you didn't bring your notes home. This is going to make things much harder."

He recognized the impatience in my voice; it made him nervous, which, in turn, made me slightly queasy. He was scared of me. I hated that. I never knew if it was a father-and-son thing or whether I, in particular, with my short temper, my inherited impatience, was the source of his anxiety. "Never mind," I said. "This'll be fun anyway. I love Latin."

"You do?" he asked eagerly (anything to get the focus off the missing notes). I watched him work for a while—his nicotine-stained fingers curled around the pen, his bad handwriting.

"How exactly do you seize and carry off a Sabine woman, Dad?" he asked me.

"I'll tell you later."

Pause. "Is *helmet* a verb?" he said.

On and on it went, the afternoon shadows spreading across the kitchen tiles. Pencil tip bouncing on the vinyl tabletop. Gradually, I became aware of a kind of hum in the room. Where was it coming from? From him? But what was it? My eyes settled on him. It was a kind of boredom, yes, but a rarefied kind, an exquisite, almost cellular conviction of the irrelevance of the task at hand. And for some odd reason, for those few seconds, I was experiencing it as if it were occurring *in my own body*.

Oh, I thought, so this is how he's going through his school day. Against *this*, you cannot win. And suddenly—it was as unmistakable as the sound of a breaking window—I understood that we had lost the school battle.

I also knew in that same instant—knew it in my blood—that I was going to lose him over this stuff, that one of these days he was going to stand up across the table and say, "Where are my notes? I'll tell you where my notes are. I shoved them up my ass. And if you don't lay the fuck off me, I'm going to shove them up yours." And then he'd be gone, slam, and that'd be that.

"Jesse," I said softly. He knew I was watching him and it made him anxious, as if he were on the verge of getting in trouble (again), and this activity, this flipping through the textbook, back and forth, back and forth, was a way of diverting it.

"Jesse, put down your pen. Stop for a second, please."

"What?" he said. He's so pale, I thought. Those cigarettes are leaching the life out of him.

I said, "I want you to do me a favor. I want you to think about whether or not you want to go to school."

"Dad, the notes are at my—"

"Never mind about the notes. I want you to think about whether or not you want to keep going to school."

"Why?"

I could feel my heart speeding up, the blood moving into my face. This was a place I'd never been to before, never even imagined before. "Because if you don't, it's all right."

"What's all right?"

Just say it, spit it out.

"If you don't want to go to school anymore, then you don't have to."

He cleared his throat. "You're going to let me quit school?"

"If you want. But please, take a few days to think about it. It's a monu—"

He got to his feet. He always got to his feet when he was excited; his long limbs couldn't endure the agitation of keeping still. Leaning his frame over the table, he lowered his voice as if afraid of being overheard. "I don't need a few days."

"Take them anyway. I insist."

Later that same evening, I braced myself with a couple of glasses of wine and called his mother at my loft (it was in an old candy factory) to break the news. She was a lanky, lovely actress, the kindest woman I've ever known. An "un-actressy" actress, if you know what I mean. But a worst-case scenarist of the first order and within only a few moments she saw him living in a cardboard box in Los Angeles.

"Do you think this has happened because he has low self-esteem?" Maggie asked.

"No," I said, "I think it's happened because he hates school."

"There has to be something wrong with him if he hates school."

"*I* hated school," I said.

"Maybe that's where he's getting it from." We went on in this vein for a while until she was in tears and I was spouting rash, sweeping generalizations that would have done Che Guevara proud.

"He's got to get a job, then," Maggie said.

"Is there any point, do you think, in substituting one activity he loathes for another?"

"What's he going to do, then?"

"I don't know."

"Maybe he could do some volunteer work," she sniffed.

I woke up in the middle of the night, my wife, Tina, stirring beside me, and wandered over to the window. The moon hung disproportionately low in the sky; it had lost its way and was waiting to be called home. What if I'm wrong? I thought. What if I'm being hip at the expense of my son and letting him ruin his life?

It's true, I thought. He's got to do something. But what? What can I get him to do that won't be a repetition of the whole school debacle? He doesn't read; he loathes sports. What does he like to do? He likes to watch movies. So did I. In fact, for a few years in my late thirties, I had been the rather glib film critic for a television show. What could we do with that?

Three days later he turned up for dinner at Le Paradis, a French restaurant with white tablecloths and heavy silverware. He was waiting for me outside, sitting on a stone balustrade, smoking a cigarette. He never liked to sit in a restaurant by himself. It made him self-conscious, everybody writing him off as a loser with no friends.

I gave him a hug, you could feel the strength in his young body, its vitality. "Let's order the wine and then have a chat."

We went in. Handshakes. Adult rituals that flattered him. Even a joke between him and the bartender about John-Boy from *The Waltons*. We sat in a slightly distracted silence, waiting for the waiter. We were both waiting on something crucial; there was nothing else to talk about till then. I let him order the wine.

"Corbière," he whispered. "That's southern France, right?"

"Right."

"A bit of barnyard?"

"That's the one."

"The Corbière, please." This to the waitress with a smile that said, I know I'm playing monkey-see, monkey-do here but I'm having fun anyway. *God, he has a beautiful smile.*

We waited till the wine arrived. "You do the honors," I said. He smelled the cork, gave the wine a clumsy whirl in his glass, and rather like a cat at an unfamiliar dish of milk, took a sip. "I can't tell," he said, his nerve abandoning him at the last moment.

"Yes, you can," I said. "Just relax. If you think it's off, it's off."

"I get nervous."

"Just smell it. You'll know. First impression is always right."

He took another smell.

"Get your nose right in there."

"It's fine," he said. The waitress sniffed the top of the bottle. "Nice to see you again, Jesse. We see your dad here all the time."

We looked around the restaurant. The elderly couple from Etobicoke was there. A dentist and his wife, their son finishing up a business degree at some college in Boston. They waved. We waved back. *What if I'm wrong?*

"So," I said, "have you been thinking about what we talked about?"

I could see he wanted to get to his feet but he couldn't. He looked around as though irritated by the constraint. Then drew his pale face close to mine as if he were divulging a secret. "The truth is," he whispered, "I don't ever want to see the inside of a school again."

My stomach fluttered. "Okay, then."

He looked at me, speechless. He was waiting for the quo in the quid pro quo.

I said, "One thing, though. You don't have to work, you don't have to pay rent. You can sleep till five every day. But no drugs. Any drugs and the deal's off."

"Okay," he said.

"I mean it. I'll drop a fucking *house* on you if you start in with that stuff."

"Okay."

"But," I said, "there's something else." (I felt like the detective in *Columbo*.)

"What?" he said.

"I want you to watch three movies a week with me. I pick them. It's the only education you're going to get."

"You're kidding," he said after a moment.

I didn't waste any time. The next afternoon, I sat him down on the blue couch in the living room, me on the right, him on the left, pulled the curtains, and showed him François Truffaut's *The 400 Blows* (1959). I figured it was a good way to slide into European art films, which I knew were going to bore him until he learned how to watch them. It's like learning a variation on regular grammar.

Truffaut, I explained (I wanted to keep it brief), came to filmmaking through the back door; he was a high school dropout (like you), a draft dodger, a small-time thief; but he adored movies and spent his childhood sneaking into the cinema houses that were all over postwar Paris.

When he was twenty years old, a sympathetic editor offered Truffaut a job writing film criticism—which led, a half-dozen years later, to making his first film. *The 400 Blows* (which in French, *Les Quatre Cente Coups*, is an idiom for "Sowing Your Wild Oats") was an autobiographical look at Truffaut's troubled early years of truancy.

To find an actor to play a teenage version of himself, the twenty-seven-year-old novice director put an ad in the newspaper. A few weeks later a dark-haired kid who'd run away from a boarding school in central France and hitchhiked to Paris turned up to audition for the role of Antoine.

His name was Jean-Pierre Léaud. (By now, I had Jesse's attention.) I mentioned that with the exception of one scene in a psychiatrist's office, the film was shot entirely without sound—that was added later—because Truffaut didn't have the money for recording equipment. I asked Jesse to watch for a famous scene where a whole class of kids disappear behind their teacher's back during a field trip through Paris; I touched lightly on a marvelous moment when the young boy, Antoine, is talking to a woman psychiatrist.

"Watch for the smile he gives when she asks him about sex," I said. "Remember, there was no script; this was totally improvised."

Just in time I caught myself starting to sound like a

dandruffy high school teacher. So I put on the movie. We went all the way to the end, that long scene where Antoine runs away from reform school; he runs through fields, past farmhouses, through apple groves, until he arrives at the dazzling ocean. It's as if he's never seen it before. Such *immensity*! It seems to stretch out forever. He goes down a bank of wooden steps; he advances across the sand and there, just where the waves start in, he pulls back slightly and looks into the camera; the film freezes; the movie's over.

After a few moments, I said, "What did you think?"

"A bit boring."

I recouped. "Do you see any parallels between Antoine's situation and yours?"

He thought about that for a second. "No."

I said, "Why do you think he has that funny expression on his face at the end of the movie, the last shot?"

"I don't know."

"How does he look?"

"He looks worried," Jesse said.

"What could he be worried about?"

"I don't know."

I said, "Look at his situation. He's run away from reform school and from his family; he's free."

"Maybe he's worried about what he's going to do now."

I said, "What do you mean?"

"Maybe he's saying, 'Okay, I've made it this far. But what's next?'"

"Okay, let me ask you again," I said. "Do you see anything in common between his situation and yours?"

He grinned. "You mean what am I going to do now that I don't have to go to school?"

"Yes."

"I don't know."

"Well, maybe that's why the kid looks worried. He doesn't know either," I said.

After a moment he said, "When I was in school, I worried about getting bad marks and getting in trouble. Now that I'm not in school, I worry that maybe I've ruined my life."

"That's good," I said.

"How is it good?"

"It means you're not going to relax into a bad life."

"I wish I could stop worrying though. Do you worry?"

I found myself taking an involuntary breath. "Yes."

"So it never stops, no matter how well you do?"

"It's about the *quality* of the worry," I said. "I have happier worries now than I used to."

He stared out the window. "This is all making me feel like having a cigarette. Then I can worry about getting lung cancer."

For dessert I gave him *Basic Instinct* (1992) with Sharon Stone the next day. Again, I offered up a little intro to the film, nothing fancy. Simple rule of thumb: Keep it bare bones. If he wants to know more, he'll ask.

I said, "Paul Verhoeven. Dutch director; came to Hollywood after a few hits in Europe. Great visual attack, exquisite lighting. Made a couple of excellent films, ultraviolent but watchable. *RoboCop* is the best of the bunch." (I was starting to sound like a Morse code machine but I didn't want to lose him.)

I went on. "He also made one of the worst films ever, a camp classic called *Showgirls*."

We started in, a tawny-skinned blonde butchering a man with an ice pick while engaged in sexual intercourse with him. Nice opening volley. After fifteen minutes it's difficult not to make the assumption that *Basic Instinct* is not just *about* sleazy people, but *by* sleazy people. There's a dirty-eared, schoolboy's fascination with cocaine and lesbian "decadence." But it's a marvelously watchable film—you have to say that. It evokes a kind of agreeable dread. Something important or nasty always seems to be happening, even when it isn't.

And then there's the dialogue. I mentioned to Jesse that the writer Joe Eszterhas, a former journalist, was paid three million dollars for this kind of stuff:

DETECTIVE: How long were you dating him?
SHARON STONE: I wasn't dating him. I was fucking him.
DETECTIVE: Are you sorry he's dead?
SHARON STONE: Yes. I liked fucking him.

Jesse couldn't take his eyes off the screen. He may have appreciated *The 400 Blows* but this was something else.

"Can we pause it for a moment?" he said and raced to the toilet for a pee; from the couch I heard the clank of the toilet seat, then a gush, as if a horse were standing in there. "Close the door, Jesse, for Pete's sake!" (We were learning all sorts of things today.) Bang, door closed. Then he hurried back, stocking feet thumping the floor, holding his pants by the waist, and vaulted back onto the couch. "You have to admit it, Dad—this is a *great* film."

CHAPTER 2

ONE DAY HE BROUGHT A GIRL HOME. Her name was Rebecca Ng, a Vietnamese knockout. "Nice to meet you, David," she said, holding my eye.

David?

"How's your day going?"

"How's my day going?" I repeated idiotically. "So far, so good."

Did I enjoy living in the neighborhood? Why, yes, thank you.

"I have an aunt who lives a few streets over," she said. "She's very nice. Old country but very nice."

Old country?

Rebecca Ng (pronounced Ning) was dressed to the nines, spotless white jeans, maroon long-collared blouse, leather jacket, Beatle boots. You had the feeling she'd paid for these clothes herself, an after-school job in a Yorkville boutique, Saturdays serving drinks to ring-removing executives in the bar of the Four Seasons Hotel (when she wasn't polishing off an early credit in calculus). As she turned her head to speak to Jesse, I caught a whiff of perfume. Delicate, expensive.

"So here we are," she said.

Then he took her downstairs to his bedroom. I opened my mouth to protest. It was a pit down there. There were no windows, no natural light. Just a bed with a ratty green blanket, clothes on the floor, CDs splashed around the room, a computer facing the wall, a "library" consisting of an autographed Elmore Leonard (unread), George Eliot's *Middlemarch* (a hopeful gift from his mother), plus a collection of hip-hop magazines with scowling black men on the cover. A collection of water glasses squatted on the night table. They cracked like a pistol shot when you pried them loose. There was also the occasional "adult" magazine (*1-800-Slut*) peeking from the space between his mattress and boxspring. "I don't have a problem with pornography," he told me matter-of-factly.

"Well, I do," I said. "So keep it hidden."

Next door in the laundry room, half the towels in the house fermented on the cement floor. But I kept quiet. I sensed that now was not the time to treat him like a child: "Why don't you kids have some milk and cookies while I get back to mowing that darn front yard!"

Soon the whump of a bass guitar rose up through the floor. You could hear Rebecca's voice floating above the music, then Jesse's voice, deeper, confident. Then bright bursts of laughter. Good, I thought. She's discovered how amusing he is.

"How *old* is that girl?" I asked when he returned from walking her to the subway.

"Sixteen," he said. "She's got a boyfriend, though."

"I can imagine."

He smiled uncertainly. "What do you mean?"

"Nothing in particular."

He looked worried.

I said, "I suppose I mean that if she's got a boyfriend, why is she over at your house?"

"She's pretty, isn't she?"

"She certainly is. She knows it too."

"Everybody likes Rebecca. They all pretend they want to be her friend. She lets them drive her around."

"How old's her boyfriend?"

"Her age. He's kind of a nerd, though."

"That speaks well for her," I said primly.

"How so?"

"It makes her more interesting," I said.

He caught a glimpse of himself in the mirror over the kitchen sink. Turning his head slightly to the side, he sucked in his cheeks, pursed his lips, and frowned gravely. This was his "mirror face." A way he never looked otherwise. You almost expected his hair, which was thick like a raccoon's, to stand up on end.

"But the guy before him was twenty-five," he said. (He wanted to talk about her.) Pulling his gaze with some difficulty from his reflection, he returned his face to its normal cast.

"Twenty-five?"

"She's got guys all over her, Dad. Like flies."

In that instant he seemed wiser than I was at his age. Less delusionally vain. (Hardly an accomplishment.) But the whole thing with Rebecca Ng made me nervous. It was like watching him get into a very expensive car. I could smell the new leather from here.

"I didn't look like I was coming on to her or anything, did I?" he asked.

"No, not at all."

"Not nervous or anything?"

"No. Were you?"

"Just when I look closely at her. The rest of the time I'm fine."

"You seemed pretty on top of things to me."

"I did, didn't I?" And again you could see a kind of lightness come into his limbs, a holiday in a minor key from that blur of worry and second-guessing to which, as if pulled by gravity, he would return. How little I can give him, I thought—just these little apple slices of reassurance, like feeding a rare animal at the zoo.

Through the wall, I could hear our neighbor Eleanor. She was rattling about in her kitchen, making tea, listening to the radio. A lonely sound. Half listening to her, half thinking about my own worries, I found myself fitfully recalling Jesse's first "date." He was ten, maybe eleven. I supervised his preparations; watched with crossed arms while he brushed his teeth, tapped his tiny underarms with my deodorant, put on a red T-shirt, brushed his hair, and set off. I followed him, ducking behind bushes and trees, staying out of sight. (How beautiful he looked in the sunlight, this little stick figure with purple hair.)

He appeared in the driveway of a towering Victorian house a few moments later with a little girl beside him. She was slightly taller than he was. I followed them to Bloor Street, where they turned into a Coffee Time, and then broke off my surveillance.

"You don't think Rebecca's out of my league, do you, Dad?" Jesse asked, catching sight of himself in the mirror, his face distorting.

"Nobody's out of your league," I said. But my heart fluttered when I said it.

I had a lot of time on my hands that winter. I was hosting a little documentary show that no one watched, but my contract was coming to an end and the executive producer had ceased returning my mildly hyperventilating e-mails. I had the uncomfortable sensation that the bottom was falling out of my television career.

"You may have to go out and look for a job just like everyone else," my wife said. That scared me. Going around hat in hand asking for work at age fifty.

"I don't think people see it like that," she said. "It's just a guy looking for work. Everybody does it."

I called a few colleagues from the old days, people who had admired (I thought) my work. But they had moved on to other shows, wives, new babies. You could sense their friendliness and at the same time your irrelevance.

I had lunch with people I hadn't seen for years. Old friends from high school, from university, from racy times in the Caribbean. Twenty minutes in, I'd look over my fork and think, I must not do this again. (I'm sure they were thinking the same thing.) How exactly, I wondered privately, am

I going to live out the rest of my life? Add five or ten years onto my present situation, it didn't look so good. My easy confidence that things were going to "sort of work out" and "end well" evaporated.

I drew up a grim little chart. Assuming no one hired me ever again, I had enough money to live for two years. Longer if I stopped going out to dinner. (Even longer if I died.) But then what? Substitute teaching? Something I hadn't done for twenty-five years. The thought made my stomach plunge. The phone ringing at six-thirty in the morning, me leaping out of bed with a racing heart and a foul taste in my mouth; into my shirt, tie, and mothbally sports jacket; the sickening subway ride to some brick school in a neighborhood I didn't know, the too-bright hallways, the vice-principal's office. "Aren't you the guy who used to be on television?" Thoughts that made you want to pour a stiff drink at eleven in the morning. Which I did a few times, followed, of course, by a Malcolm Lowry–like hangover. *You have mismanaged your life.*

Waking too early one morning, I wandered into an unfamiliar restaurant. When the bill came, it was absurdly low; obviously a mistake had been made and I didn't want it taken from the waitress's tips. I signaled her over. "This seems a little on the inexpensive side," I said.

She looked at the bill. "No, no," she replied sunnily, "that's the Senior's Special."

The Senior's Special—for the sixty-five-and-up crowd. Even more pathetic, I experienced a wave of mild gratitude. I had, after all, saved almost two dollars and fifty cents on the Ham'Eggs Early Bird.

Outside the gloom gathered. It started to snow; soggy flakes slid down the windowpanes. The little parking lot across the street disappeared in the mist. You could see a pair of red taillights moving around, somebody backing into place. Just then Jesse's mother, Maggie Huculak (pronounced Hoo-shoo-lack), phoned. She had just poured herself a glass of red wine in my loft and wanted company. The streetlights came on; the mist glowed magically around the lamps. Suddenly it was a cozy, perfect evening for two parents to talk about an adored child—his diet (poor), exercise (none), his smoking (distressing), Rebecca Ng (trouble), drugs (none that we knew of), reading (nil), movies (Hitchcock's *North by Northwest* today), drinking (at parties), the nature of his soul (dreamy).

And while we spoke I was again struck by the fact that we loved each other. Not in a carnal or romantic way—that was behind us—but something more profound. (As a young man I didn't believe that anything more profound *could* exist.) We took such pleasure in each other's company, in the reassuring sound of each other's voice. Besides which, I had learned the hard way that there was no one else on earth *except* her with whom I could talk about my son in the lavish detail I wanted to—what he said this morning, how clever it was, how handsome he looked in his new rugby shirt. ("You're exactly right! He's *very* suited to dark colors!")

No one else could endure listening to this stuff for more than thirty seconds without leaping out the window. How sad, I thought—what a waste for those parents whose loathing for each other had so hardened that it deprived them of this kind of delicious exchange.

"Do you have a boyfriend these days?" I asked.

"No," Maggie said. "No cute guys."

"You'll get one. I know you."

"I don't know," she said. "Somebody told me a few days ago that it was more likely that a woman my age would get killed in a terrorist attack than get married."

"That's a nice thing to tell you. Who said that?" I asked.

She mentioned a duck-faced actress she was rehearsing *Hedda Gabler* with.

"We did a read-through of the play, and at the end, the director, this guy I've known for years, said, 'Maggie, you are like single-malt scotch.' "

"Yeah?"

"And you know what she said?"

"What?"

"She said, 'That's the *cheap* kind, isn't it?' "

After a moment, I said, "You're a better actor than she is, Maggie; she'll never forgive you for it."

"You always say such nice things to me," she said. Her voice wobbled. She cried easily.

———————

I can't remember exactly. It may have been the same foggy night or maybe a few nights later that Rebecca Ng telephoned near four in the morning. The ring insinuated itself so perfectly into my dream (summer cottage, my mother making me a tomato sandwich in the kitchen, all of it long gone) that I didn't wake up at first. Then it rang and rang again and I picked up. It was so late, so weird for a girl her age to be up, much less calling around. "It's too late for all this, Rebecca, way too late," I said.

"Sorry," she said in a not-very-sorry voice. "I thought Jesse had his own phone."

"Even if he did—" I began, but my tongue wouldn't work. I sounded like a stroke victim.

You don't attack a teenager first thing in the morning, you wait till he's brushed his teeth, washed his face, come upstairs, sat down, and eaten his scrambled eggs. Then you do it. Then you say, "What the hell was that all about last night?"

"She had a dream about me." He tried to tone down his excitement but he had the glow of a man who has just won a big hand at poker.

"She told you that?"

"She told *him* that."

"Who?"

"Her boyfriend."

"She told her boyfriend she had a dream about you?"

"Yes." (This was beginning to sound like a Harold Pinter play.)

"Jesus."

"What?" he said, alarmed.

"Jesse, when a woman tells you she's had a dream about you, you know what's going on, don't you?"

"What?" He knew the answer. He just wanted to hear it.

"It means she likes you. It's her way of telling you that you're on her mind. *Really* on her mind."

"It's true. I think she likes me."

"I have no doubt about that. *I* like you too—" I stopped, out of words.

"But what?"

I said, "It's sneaky, that's all. And cruel. How would you like it if your girlfriend told you she had a dream about another guy?"

"She wouldn't."

"You mean if she were with you, she'd never dream about another guy?"

"Yes," he said, not entirely convinced.

I went on. "The point I'm trying to make, Jesse, is the way a girl treats her former boyfriend is the way she'll treat you."

"You figure?"

"I don't figure. I *know*. Look at your mom; she's always been kind and generous about her old boyfriends. That's why she didn't poison your ear or drag me through court."

"She wouldn't do that."

"That's precisely the point I'm making. If she wouldn't do it to *another* guy, she wouldn't do it to me. That's why I had you with her, not with somebody else."

"You knew you were going to break up?"

"I mean that it's all right to go to bed with an asshole but don't ever have a baby with one."

That shut him up.

———————————

I've kept the list of the movies we watched (yellow cards on the fridge), so I know that in the first few weeks I showed him *Crimes and Misdemeanors* (1989). There's a sort of *rushed-homework* feel to Woody Allen's movies these days, as if he's trying to get them finished and out of the way so he can move on to something else. That something else, distressingly, is another movie. It's a downward spiral. But still, after making more than thirty films, maybe he's done his life's work; maybe he's entitled to cruise on whatever gas he wants from here on in.

Yet there was a time when he knocked off beauties, one after the other. *Crimes and Misdemeanors* is a film many people have seen once but, rather like Chekhov's short stories, don't really get all of it the first time by. I've always thought it was a movie that lets you see how Woody Allen sees the world—as a place where people like your neighbors really *do* get away with murder and goofs end up with great girlfriends.

I alerted Jesse to the film's skillful storytelling, how efficiently it covers the courtship between the ophthalmologist (Martin Landau) and his hysterical girlfriend (Angelica Huston). Just a few brushstrokes and we understand how far they've come, from a delirious courtship to a murderous juncture.

What did Jesse think of it? He said, "I think I'd like Woody Allen in real life." And we left it at that.

Next I showed him a documentary, *Volcano: An Inquiry into the Life and Death of Malcolm Lowry* (1976). You can say this only once, so here it is: *Volcano* is the best documentary I've ever seen in my life. When I first started in television more than twenty years ago, I asked a senior producer if she'd heard of it.

"Are you kidding?" she said. "That's the reason I got into

television." She could even quote from it. " 'How, unless you drink as I do, can you hope to understand the beauty of an old woman from Tarasco who plays dominoes at seven o'clock in the morning.' "

What a tale the film tells: Malcolm Lowry, a rich boy, leaves England at twenty-five, drinks his way around the world, settling in Mexico, where he begins a short story. Ten years and a million drinks later, he has expanded that story into the greatest novel ever written about drinking, *Under the Volcano*, and almost driven himself insane in the process. (Strangely enough, most of the novel was written in a small cabin ten miles north of Vancouver.)

There are some writers, I explain, whose lives and deaths inspire as much curiosity and admiration as what they actually wrote. I mention Virginia Woolf (death by drowning), Sylvia Plath (death by gas), F. Scott Fitzgerald (drank himself silly and died too young). Malcolm Lowry is another. His novel is one of literature's most romantic paeans to self-destruction.

"It is scary," I told Jesse, "to imagine how many young men your age have gotten drunk and looked in the mirror and thought they saw Malcolm Lowry looking back at them. How many young men thought they were doing something more important, more poetic than just getting really smashed." I read Jesse a passage from the novel to show him why. "And this is how I sometimes think of myself," Lowry wrote, "as a great explorer who has discovered some extraordinary land from which he can never return to give his knowledge to the world: but the name of this land is hell."

"Jesus," Jesse said, slumping back into the couch. "Do you think he meant it, that he really *saw* himself that way?"

"I do."

After a moment's thought, he said, "It's not supposed to, I know, but in a strange way it makes you want to go out and get completely wrecked." I then asked him to pay special attention to the writing in the documentary, which often matches the stature of Lowry's own prose. Here's a sample, Canadian filmmaker Donald Brittain's description of Lowry's incarceration in a New York insane asylum: "This was no longer the rich bourgeois world where one fell about on soft lawns. Here were things that kept on living despite the fact they were beyond repair."

"Do you think I'm too young to read Lowry?" he asked.

Tough question. I knew that at this juncture of his life the book would lose him after twenty pages. "You need to know about some *other* books before you read him," I said.

"Which ones?"

"That's what you go to college for," I said.

"But can't you read them anyway?"

"You can. But people don't. Some books you read only if you're forced to. That's the beauty of a formal education. It makes you read a lot of stuff you'd normally never bother with."

"And that's a good thing?"

"In the end, yes."

Occasionally Tina arrived home from work to observe me luring Jesse up the stairs with a croissant in my fingers—as if I were training a porpoise at Sea World.

"He has very understanding parents," she said. Having

worked summers, holidays, even weekends, to help put herself through college, she must have found this afternoon ritual somewhat galling.

A word or two about Tina. The first time I saw her hurrying through the newsroom—this was almost fifteen years before—I thought, "Too pretty. Forget it."

We had, nevertheless, a brief flirtation that she terminated after a few weeks with the stern observation that while I was "fun to drink with," I was not "boyfriend material."

"At my age," she said, "I can't afford to find myself down the road in two years with a dead-end relationship."

Several years went by. I was leaving my bank one afternoon in an underground mall when I ran into her at the foot of the escalator. Time had lengthened her face and she looked slightly haggard. An unhappy love affair, I hoped. I tried again. We had a few dates here and there, and then one evening, walking home from somewhere, I looked over at her silhouette and thought, I must marry this woman. It was as if some mechanism for self-preservation clicked on, like a furnace on a cold night. Marry this woman, it said, and you will die happy.

On hearing the news, Maggie took me aside and whispered, "You must not blow this one."

Next I showed Jesse *Citizen Kane* (1941)—"Pretty good but no way the best film ever made"; John Huston's *The Night of the Iguana* (1964)—"Bullshit." Then *On the Waterfront* (1954).

I started with a rhetorical question. Was Marlon Brando the greatest film actor ever?

Then I did my pitch. I explained that *On the Waterfront*

appeared to be about cleaning up corruption on the New York docks, but what it was *really* about was the accelerating emergence of a new form of acting style in American movies, the Method. The results, where actors personalized a character by connecting it to real-life experience, could be overpersonal and wanky, but here they were divine.

I went on to explain that there were a number of ways you could look at the film. (It won eight Oscars.) On a literal level, it's an exciting story about a young man (Brando) who is faced with a real crisis of conscience. Does he allow evil to go unpunished, even though it's been committed by his friends? Or does he speak up?

But there was another way to view it. The film's director, Elia Kazan, made one of those awful life mistakes that stays with you forever: He was a voluntary witness before Senator Joseph McCarthy's House Un-American Activities Committee in the fifties. During the Committee's "investigations," I explained, actors and writers and directors were routinely blacklisted for being members of the Communist Party; lives were ruined.

Kazan got the nickname "Loose-lips Kazan" for his hand-licking performance and his willingness to "name names." Critics claimed *On the Waterfront* was in essence an artful justification for ratting on your friends.

I could see Jesse's eyes clouding over so I wrapped up by asking him to watch for a scene with Marlon Brando and Eva Marie Saint in a park; he takes her glove, puts it on; she wants to leave, but can't as long as he has it. When Kazan talked about Brando, he always talked about that moment. "Have you *seen* it?" he used to ask interviewers in the voice of a man who has witnessed, firsthand, an event that should not be able to take place in the natural world—but has.

On it went. I showed *Who's Afraid of Virginia Woolf?* (1966); *Plenty* (1985) with Meryl Streep. Graham Greene's *The Third Man* (1949). Some of the films Jesse liked, some bored him. But it beat paying rent and having to get a job. I got a surprise when I showed him *A Hard Day's Night* (1964).

It's hard for someone who didn't grow up in the early sixties, I said, to imagine how important the Beatles were. Barely out of their teens, they were treated like Roman emperors everywhere they went. They had the extraordinary quality of making you feel as if, in spite of their hysterical popularity, you alone understood how great they were, that they were somehow your own private discovery.

I told Jesse about seeing them at Maple Leaf Gardens in Toronto in 1966. I've never seen anything like it, the screams, the explosion of flashbulbs, John Lennon hamming his way through "Long Tall Sally." The teenage girl next to me snatched so violently at my binoculars she almost took my head with them.

I told him about interviewing George Harrison in 1989 when he released his last album; how, waiting in his office at Handmade Films, I had almost passed out when I turned around and there he was, a slim, middle-aged man with thick black hair. "Just a minute," he said in that accent you heard on *The Ed Sullivan Show*. "I've got to comb my hair."

I told Jesse how "right" they got it when they made *A Hard Day's Night*—from shooting in gleaming black-and-white, to getting the boys to wear the trend-setting black suits with white shirts, to the use of hand-held cameras to give the movie a documentary, real-life feel. That jiggly six o'clock–news style influenced a generation of filmmakers.

I pointed him toward a few delightful snippets: George Harrison (the best actor of the bunch, according to the director Richard Lester) and the scene with the awful shirts; John Lennon snorting at the top of a Coca-Cola bottle in the train. (Few people got the joke then.) But my favorite part, easily, is the Beatles running down a flight of stairs and bursting outdoors into an open field. With "Can't Buy Me Love" soaring in the background, it is a moment so irresistible, so ecstatic, that it fills me, even to this day, with the feeling of being near to—but unable to possess—something profoundly important. After all these years, I still don't know what that "something" is but I feel its presence when I watch this movie.

Just before I put the film on, I mentioned that in 2001 the remaining Beatles released a collection of the group's number-one hits. It went straight to the top of the charts in *thirty-four different countries.* Canada, the United States, Iceland, all over Europe. This from a band that had broken up thirty-one years before.

Then I said what I'd wanted to say all my life: "Ladies and gentlemen, the Beatles!"

Jesse watched the film in polite silence, at the end of which he said simply, "Dreadful." He went on. "And John Lennon was the worst of the bunch." (Here he mimicked Lennon with astonishing accuracy.) "A totally embarrassing man."

I was speechless. The music, the film, its look, its style . . . But most of all, it was the fucking Beatles!

"Indulge me for a second, okay?" I said. I fished around

among my Beatles CDs until I found "It's Only Love" on
the *Rubber Soul* CD. I put it on and played it for him (my
finger raised to capture his attention should it meander for
a millisecond).

"Wait, wait," I cried ecstatically. "Wait for the hook! Listen to that voice, it's like barbed wire!"

Over the music I shouted, "Is that not simply the best
voice, ever, in rock and roll?"

At the song's conclusion, I subsided into my seat. After
a religious pause and in a voice grasping for normalcy (it
still kills me, that middle-eight), I said, "So what do you
think?"

"They've got good voices."

Good voices?

"But how does it make you *feel*?" I cried.

Appraising me cautiously with his mother's eyes, he said,
"Honestly?"

"Honestly."

"Nothing." Pause. "I feel nothing at all." He placed a con-
ciliatory hand on my shoulder. "I'm sorry, Dad."

Was there a look of concealed amusement on his lips?
Had I turned into a ranting old coot already?

CHAPTER 3

LATE ONE AFTERNOON—it was nearly six o'clock—Jesse still hadn't appeared. I went down the stairs and knocked on his door.

"Jesse," I said. "Can I come in?"

He was lying on his side under the blankets, facing the wall. I turned on the bedside lamp and sat down gingerly on the edge of the bed.

"I got you something to eat," I said.

He turned over. "I can't eat, Dad, really."

I took out a croissant. "I'm just going to have a little bite myself, then."

He looked hungrily at the bag.

"So," I said (munch, munch), "what's up?"

"Nothing," he said.

"Is this about Rebecca?" I said.

He sat bolt upright, his thick hair standing on end like he'd been hit by lightning. "She had an orgasm," he whispered. I recoiled. I couldn't help myself. This wasn't the sort of conversation I wanted to have with my sixteen-year-old son, not in that detail anyway. (That's what his buddies were for.) But I could also see that having said those words, just by getting them to the surface and into the light, he had released a dose of poison from his body.

I hid my discomfort by taking a large mouthful of dough almost whole.

"But you know what she said afterward?" he said.

"No, I don't."

"She said, 'I really like you, Jesse, but when I hug you, it's like hugging a friend.' "

"She said that?"

"Exactly. I swear, Dad. Like I was some kind of girlfriend or gay or something."

After a moment I said, "You know what I think?"

"What?" He looked like a convicted man waiting to hear his sentence.

I said, "I think she's a troublemaking little bitch who loves to torment you."

"Really?"

"Really."

He lay back as if the awfulness of the situation had just reoccurred to him.

"Listen to me," I said. "I'm going to have to go out pretty soon. I've got some things to do and you're going to start thinking about this stuff again . . ."

"Probably."

Weighing my words, I spoke carefully. "I don't want to have an inappropriate conversation with you—we're not pals, we're father and son—but I want to say this to you. Girls don't have orgasms with people they're not physically attracted to."

"Are you sure?"

"Yes," I said emphatically.

(Is that true? I wondered. Doesn't matter. Not today's problem.)

I took Jesse to see *Sexy Beast* (2002) with Ben Kingsley at the Cumberland theater. I could tell he wasn't watching the movie, that he was sitting there in the dark thinking about Rebecca Ng and that "hugging a friend" business. On the way home, I said, "Did you get a chance to talk about all the stuff you wanted to talk about today?"

He didn't look at me. "Absolutely," he said. Door closed; mind your own beeswax. We walked the rest of the way to the subway in a curiously uncomfortable silence. We'd never before had a problem with talking, but now it seemed as if we'd run out of things to say to each other. Perhaps, even at his young age, he intuited I couldn't tell him anything that was going to make a difference. Only Rebecca could do that. But it seemed he'd forgotten how his own nervous system worked, that just putting things to words released him, partially, from the distress they described. He was sealed off from me. And I felt a curious reluctance to barge into rooms where I wasn't invited. He was growing up.

The weather, the way it always is when you're heartbroken, was terrible. Rainy mornings, colorless skies in the afternoon. A car had squashed a squirrel in front of the door and you couldn't go in or out of the house without looking, involuntarily, at the furry gore. At a family dinner with his mother and my wife, Tina, he fidgeted with his steak and mashed potatoes (his favorite) with polite, if slightly mechanical, enthusiasm. He looked wan, like a sick child, and drank too much wine. It wasn't so much the quantity actually; it was the *way* he drank it, too fast, chasing a sensation. Something you see in older drinkers. I thought, We'll have to keep an eye on this.

Looking at him across the table, I found myself moving fitfully from one unhappy image to another. I saw him as an older man driving a taxi around town on a rainy night, the car stinking of marijuana, a tabloid newspaper folded on the seat beside him. *I told him he could do whatever the hell he pleases; forget the rent, sleep all day. How cool a dad am I!*

But what if nothing happened? What if I had dropped him down a well from which there was no door, no exit, just a succession of shitty jobs and shitty employers and no money and too much booze? What if I had set the stage for all that?

I found him alone on the porch later that night. "You know," I said, settling into the wicker chair beside him, "this thing you're doing, not going to school, it's a hard route— you know that."

"I know that," he said.

I went on. "I just want to make really sure that you know what you're doing, that there are real consequences to having only a grade-ten education."

"I know," he said, "but I think I'm going to have a good life anyway."

"You do?"

"Yep. Don't you?"

"Don't I what?"

"Think I'm goi

I looked over a

and I thought I'd s

heart.

"I think you're g

ter of fact, I'm sure

And when he takes his lea

dling with a long piece of

trick.

"Now watch thi

what he does

desk. It's li

It's

of

It was a spring af

around five. I was goi

was the deal. I had a ..... with

somebody about a m___ job (money still hemorrhaging), but I thought I'd get him started on a movie and then leave. I put on *Giant* (1956), with James Dean as a young cowboy. Jesse munched a croissant as the credits rolled over the big-cattle country, breathing through his nose, which kind of irritated me.

"Who's that?" he said. Munch, munch.

"James Dean."

Pause. "Cool-looking guy."

We were coming up on that scene where Rock Hudson is trying to talk the fox-featured Dean into selling a tiny piece of property that he's just inherited. There are three or four other men in the room, businessmen, pressed white shirts and ties, all wanting the same thing, wanting this punk to sell. (They suspect there's oil nearby.) Hudson offers him a wad of money. No, says the cowboy, he's sorry but he kinda likes having a piece of land all his own. Not much, but mine.

ve, he stops by the door, fid-
rope, like he's practicing a rodeo

s," I said. "Watch how he leaves the room,
with his hand, like he's sweeping snow off a
ke he's saying, 'Fuck you,' to the business guys."
one of those moments at the movies, so odd, so out-
the-blue, that the first time you see it, you can't quite believe your eyes.

"Wow!" Jesse said, sitting up. "Can we watch that again?"
(Awe may be the appropriate sentiment when considering
Anton Chekhov, but "Wow!" is definitely the right call for
James Dean.)

A few minutes later, I had to go out. On the way out the
door I said, "You should watch the rest of this—you'll like
it." Which I imagined, rather self-congratulatorily, he would.
But when I came back later that night (eleven dollars for the
taxi, no job), I found him sitting at the kitchen table eating a
bowl of spaghetti. Eating with his mouth open. I'd told him
a dozen times not to do that. It annoyed me that his mother
had let it go at her end. You're not doing a young guy a favor
letting him have bad table manners. I said, "Jesse, close your
mouth, please, when you're chewing."

"Sorry."

"We've been over this before."

"I only do it at home," he said. I was going to ignore that
but I couldn't. "If you do it at home, you're going to forget
not to do it when you're out."

"Okay," he said.

I said, "So what did you think of it?"

"What?"

"Giant."

"Oh, I took it off."

After a moment I said, "You know, Jesse, you're not doing very much these days. You really ought to stick out a movie like *Giant*. It's the only education you're getting."

Neither of us said anything while I looked for a way out of the little box of self-righteousness I had painted myself into. "Do you know who Dennis Hopper is?" I said.

"The guy in *Apocalypse Now*."

"I interviewed him once. I asked him who his favorite actor was. I thought he was going to say Marlon Brando. Everyone says Marlon Brando. But he didn't. He said James Dean. You know what else he said? He said the best piece of acting he'd ever seen in his life was that scene with James Dean and the rope."

"You're kidding."

"Seriously." I waited a moment. I said, "You know the story with James Dean, eh? Made three movies and then died in a car accident."

"How old was he?"

"Early twenties."

"Was he drunk?"

"No, just going too fast. *Giant* was his last movie. He never got to see it."

He thought about that for a second. "Who do *you* think is the greatest actor, Dad?"

"Brando," I said. "That scene in *On the Waterfront*. Totally improvised when Brando takes the girl's glove and puts it on his hand. That's as good as it gets. We should watch it again."

I went on to say, to repeat, rather, what my betters had told me in university: that the second time you see something is really the *first* time. You need to know how it ends before you can appreciate how beautifully it's put together from the beginning.

He didn't know what to say—he was still in the doghouse about *Giant*—so he said, "Sure."

I picked the movies arbitrarily, in no particular order; for the most part they had to be good, classics when possible, but engaging, had to pull him out of his own thoughts with a strong storyline. There was no point, not at this juncture anyway, in showing him stuff like Fellini's *8½* (1963). They would come in time, those films. (Or they wouldn't.) What I wasn't prepared to be was impervious to his pleasure, to his appetite to be entertained. You have to start somewhere; if you want to excite someone about literature, you don't start by giving him *Ulysses*—although, to be candid, a life without *Ulysses* seems like just a fine idea to me.

The next day I settled on Alfred Hitchcock's *Notorious* (1946), for my money, the best Hitchcock film ever. Ingrid Bergman, never more beautiful, never more vulnerable, plays the daughter of a German spy who is "loaned" to a pack of South America–based Nazis. Cary Grant plays her American controller, who falls in love with her even while sending her off to marry the ringleader. His bitterness, her faint hopes that he'll call off the plan and marry her himself, give the story tremendous romantic tension. But mostly it's a classic suspense yarn. Will the Nazis find out what Bergman's real mission is? Will Grant arrive in time to save her? The last five minutes leave you gasping the first time through.

I opened things up with a brief introduction to Hitchcock, Jesse as always on the left hand side of the couch, a coffee in his hand. I said that Hitchcock was an English director, a bit of a prick with a mildly unhealthy thing for some of the blond actresses in his films. (I wanted to capture his attention.) I went on to say that he made a half-dozen masterpieces, adding, unnecessarily, that anyone who didn't agree with that probably didn't love movies. I asked him to look for a couple of things in the film. The staircase inside the villain's house in Rio de Janeiro. How long was it? How long would it take to go down it? I didn't tell him why.

I asked him also to listen to the graceful, sometimes suggestive dialogue, to remember that this film was made in 1946. I asked him to watch for a very famous camera shot that starts at the top of a ballroom and slowly descends into a group of partygoers until it arrives, tight, on the clenched hand of Ingrid Bergman. What is she holding? (A key to the wine cellar where the evidence of the Nazi mischief is disguised in wine bottles.)

I went on to say that a number of distinguished critics maintain that Cary Grant may well have been the best actor, *ever,* in films, because he could "embody good and evil simultaneously."

"You know what 'simultaneously' means?" I said.

"Yeah, yeah."

I showed him an article that Pauline Kael wrote about

Grant in *The New Yorker.* "He may not be able to do much," Kael wrote, "but what he can do no one else has ever done so well, and because of his civilized nonaggressiveness and his witty acceptance of his own foolishness we see ourselves idealized in him."

Then I did what I wish all my high school teachers had done more often. I shut up and put the movie on.

While a construction crew worked on the church across the street (they were making it over into a luxury condominium), this is what we heard:

INGRID BERGMAN (kissing Grant): This is a very strange love affair.

GRANT: Why?

BERGMAN: Maybe the fact that you don't love me.

GRANT: When I don't love you, I'll let you know.

Jesse looked over at me a few times, smiling, nodding, getting it. We went onto the porch after; he wanted a cigarette. We watched the construction crew for a while.

"So, what did you think?" I asked in an offhand voice.

"Good." Puff, puff. Hammer, hammer across the street.

"Did you happen to notice the stairway in the house?"

"Yeah."

"Did you notice it at the *end* of the movie? When Cary Grant and Bergman are trying to leave the house and we don't know if they're going to get away or not?"

He looked caught out. "No, I didn't."

"They're *longer,*" I said. "Hitchcock built a second set of stairs for that final scene. You know why he did that?"

"Why?"

"Because that way it would take longer to get down them. Do you know why he wanted that?"

"To make it more suspenseful?"

"Can you guess now what Hitchcock is famous for?"

"Suspense?"

I knew enough to stop right there. I thought, You taught him something today. Don't kill it. I said, "That's all for now; school's out."

Was that gratitude I saw on his young features? I got out of the chair and went to go inside. "One thing though, Dad," he said. "That shot that's so well known, the one at the party when Ingrid Bergman has the key in her hand?"

"Everybody who goes to film school studies it," I said.

"It's an okay shot," he said. "But to be honest it didn't really strike me as that special."

"Really?" I said.

"What about you?"

I thought about it for a second. "Me neither," I said, and went inside.

CHAPTER 4

JESSE GOT A GIRLFRIEND, Claire Brinkman; she was a freckle-faced, upbeat charmer who adored her parents, liked going to school, was president of the classical music club, performed in amateur theater, played field hockey, whipped around the city on in-line skates, and may well, I worried, have disqualified herself from Jesse's imagination because she didn't fuck him around enough. Besides, you can't compete with a ghost, and the ghost of Rebecca Ng crashed around the house at night like a poltergeist.

That June we went to Cuba, the three of us, Maggie, Jesse, and me. A divorced couple taking a holiday with their beloved son. My wife, being the only one with a regular job, stayed at Maggie's. To outsiders or to her occasionally unforgiving friends, it must have sounded a tad peculiar, this family trip, but Tina understood it, understood that the days of Maggie and me sneaking into each other's bed were long behind us. Still, the fact of her remaining behind in my ex-wife's house while the rest of us tootled off to the Caribbean—how odd life can be.

It was a last-minute thing. Just when I'd given up the ghost, when I'd spent a few minutes that very morning kicking impotently at the furniture and bleating my unemployment woes at Tina (the job at the documentary channel having floated, dead, to the surface), I got a message on the answering service. It was from a tubby, beet-faced, passive-aggressive South African named Derek H. He was producing an hour-long documentary on, get this, Viagra, and wanted to know if I was interested in "fronting" it. Fifteen thousand bucks, travel to Philadelphia and New York with a few weeks in Bangkok, where, according to Derek, old men were literally "fucking themselves to death."

We "took a meeting," I met the crew, picked out a hotel by the river in Bangkok, and discussed a timetable. Early July. Shook hands all around. I went out that night, got ecstatically, knee-walking drunk, and dreamed up the idea of Jesse, his mom, and me going to Cuba.

Departure day, Claire Brinkman came by on her skates to say good-bye; she got there just before the limo arrived. Her red-rimmed eyes worried me.

We took a couple of fancy rooms in the Hotel Parque Central in Old Havana. Swimming pool on the roof, fat dressing gowns in the cupboard, a Roman-banquet buffet every morning. The expense made Maggie nervous—she was a prairie farm girl whose heart fluttered if a long-distance call went more than a minute—but I insisted. Besides, how many more trips did we have with our son? How much longer would he want to travel with his parents?

It happened on our third night there. That day I'd taken Jesse to the Museum of the Revolution, looked at the boat that Castro and his eighty-two revolutionaries sneaked back to Cuba in, saw a photo of the dead Che Guevara; had a boozy dinner on the balcony of a private residence overlooking the Prado; stumbled down Calle Obispo for a mojito nightcap, the three of us, a band flailing and wailing in the boxy, fly-specked room; and then, my eyes closing from the heat and the booze, we returned to the hotel. It was nearly three in the morning. Maggie went to her room. Jesse and I watched television for a while. Then it was snoozy time.

"Can I keep the TV on with the sound down?" he asked.

"Why don't you read something instead?" I said.

We turned out the light; I could feel him lying there, awake, restless. Finally I turned the light on. "Jesse!"

He couldn't sleep. He was too excited. Could he go out and have a cigarette? Right over there, just across the street, that bench on the edge of the park? You can see it from here, Dad. Finally I agreed.

He dressed quickly and hurried out. I lay there for a few moments, turned off the light, then turned it on. Got up and went over to the window and opened it. The air-conditioning stopped. The room went silent. Suddenly you could hear everything very clearly, cicadas, a few voices in Spanish, a car slowly cruising. A room-service cart passed by in the hallway outside the door, cups rattling.

I stood by the window, looking out over the dark park.

Figures moved in the shadows. Hookers walked slowly through the trees, had a cigarette by the statue. Just beyond was the dome of the Museum of the Revolution.

Jesse stepped into my view on the sidewalk below, baggy pants, turned-around baseball hat. He lit a cigarette as if he were in a movie, looked this way and that (I caught a glance of his mirror face), and then started across the street to the park bench. I was just about to yell down to be careful when a dark-skinned man in a yellow shirt came out of the darkness. He made straight for Jesse, his hand extended. I waited to see if Jesse would shake it. He did. Mistake. Two other Cubans materialized, smiling, nodding, standing too close. Pointing up the street. Incredibly (I could hardly believe my eyes), they headed off with Jesse in between them, diagonally across the park.

I put on my clothes and took the elevator down to the lobby. Big, high-ceilinged room, marble floors, chilly as a skating rink, canned music, a couple of security guys in gray suits and hand-held radios by the front door. They gave me a salute and buzzed open the door for me. The hot air hit me outside.

I crossed the street and stepped into the park. A hooker picked up on me. She rose like smoke from a park bench and drifted across to me. I said no thank you, and went through the park, looking here and there, for Jesse. He must have headed down some side street with his new pals. But which one?

I was moving down the east side of the park, near the taxis and three-wheeled *cocos*, when I noticed, through the vegetation, a street heading alongside the city's grand theater. A bright light at the end. I followed it down till I came to the front of an open-air bar. The place was empty, except for Jesse having a beer, the three hustlers sitting close to him at the same table. He had a sort of worried look on his face as if it were starting to occur to him that maybe something wasn't quite right here. I went over. "Can I speak to you for a second?"

The hustler in the yellow shirt said, "You his daddy?"

"Yes."

I said to Jesse, "I have to speak to you."

"Yeah, sure," he said and scrambled to his feet. Yellow Shirt followed him out into the street, hovered nearby, trying to hear. I said, "These guys aren't your friends."

"I'm just having a beer."

I said, "You're going to end up paying for a whole lot more than a beer. You buy these guys anything?"

"Not yet."

The owner came out from the bar, a squat guy, very calm. Not surprised by any of this. He came over to Jesse and took him by the shirtsleeve.

I said, "What are you doing?"

The guy didn't answer. He just kept walking back to the bar, holding on to Jesse's shirt. I could feel my heart starting to thump unhealthily. Here we go. Fuck, here we go.

I said to him in Spanish, "How much does he owe you?"

He had Jesse back in the bar now. He said, "Ten dollars."

I said, "That's pretty expensive for a beer."

"That's the price."

"Here," I said, and put an American five on the table. "Let's go."

But the owner said, "He ordered a rum. I've already made it."

I said, "You mean you've already *poured* it?"

"Same thing."

I said to Jesse, "You touch that drink?"

Jesse shook his head, scared now.

I said, "Follow me," and we started back up the street. The hustlers came out after us. One of them came around and stood in front of me. He said, "He ordered a drink. Now he has to pay."

I tried to step around him but he stepped in front of me.

I said, "I'm going to call the cops."

The hustler said, "Okay, fine." But he stepped back.

We kept walking, the hustler bobbing around, pulling at my sleeve, his friends following behind, me saying to Jesse, "No matter what happens, keep walking." We went across the park, almost running now, Jesse sticking very close to me, and then, when we could see the hotel doors, I said, "Run."

We ran across the street and under the façade and in through the night door. But they came in after us, into the lobby. Still moving, I said to the guy in the yellow shirt, "You better get the fuck out of here." But he wasn't afraid of anything. The elevator door opened; he tried to squeeze in with me and Jesse, his pals hanging back in the lobby.

The security guys came out of nowhere. There was a commotion in Spanish, the doors shut. We went up three floors, Jesse saying nothing. Throwing me little worried glances. Looking at himself in the mirror, making that face again. He thought I was pissed off at him, which I was, abstractly, but what he didn't know was that I was experiencing a kind of elation. I had, corny as it sounds, gotten on my horse and ridden out to save him. Served him well, protected him, done my job. I was, in fact, privately happy at how things had turned out. After a certain age you don't get to do that much for your children; you've got all that juice and not enough to do with it.

We were too jacked up to go to bed or to watch television. To be honest, I was dying for a drink. "Maybe we should go see if we can get a beer," I said.

We waited ten or fifteen minutes and peeked out the hotel door; no sign of Yellow Shirt. We hurried along the near edge of the park, past the shopping plaza to the Calle Obispo, and headed down the narrow street toward the ocean. The old city hung in a silent ball of heat. "That's where Ernest Hemingway used to drink," I said as we passed the darkened El Floridita. "It's a tourist trap now, ten bucks a beer, but back in the fifties, it was supposed to be the best bar in town."

We passed a couple of caged-up cafés, places that had been screeching with life and strumming guitars and cigar smoke a few hours earlier. Then an old-fashioned drugstore, dark wood, row upon row of clay jars along the back wall.

Soon we were standing outside Hemingway's old hotel, the Ambos Mundos, at the foot of the street. "He wrote some of his worst stuff up there on the fifth floor," I said.

"Is he worth reading?" Jesse asked.

"What the *hell* were you thinking back there, Jesse?" I said. "Going off with those hustlers like that?"

He didn't answer. You could see he was racing around inside his head, ripping open doors and cupboards, looking for the right thing to say.

"Tell me," I said gently.

"I thought I was having an adventure. Smoking a cigarette and drinking rum in a foreign city. You know?"

"Didn't you feel like there was something off, those guys being so friendly at three in the morning?"

"I didn't want to hurt their feelings," he said. (How young he still is, I thought. That tall body, that good vocabulary. It can fool you.)

"Those guys are used to making people feel guilty. They do it all day long. It's their job."

We walked awhile longer down the street. Yellow lamps overhead, balconies looking down, laundry hanging motionless, like people waiting. "If you're going to read Hemingway," I said, "read *The Sun Also Rises*. A few of his short stories too. The rest gets a bit nutty." I looked around. You could smell the odor of decaying masonry, hear the ocean smashing against the seawall on the other side of the Avenida del Puerto. But no bar. "They say you can get anything anytime in Havana," I said, "but apparently not."

Inside the Ambos Mundos hotel, you could see the night clerk talking to a pretty girl.

We followed a narrow cobblestone street east, the crumbling pastel apartment buildings rising on both sides, thick vines trailing down, a bright full moon shining overhead; no stars, just this single bright coin in the middle of a black sky. Night was at its peak. We came out into a square, a dirty-brown cathedral squatting at one end, a lighted café on the other, three or four tables sitting near the middle of the square. We sat down. A white-jacketed waiter disengaged himself from the brightly lit interior and came over.

"*¿Señores?*"

"*Dos cervezas, por favor.*"

Out they came, two ice-cold beers at four o'clock in the morning.

"I'm sorry about that business back at the hotel," Jesse said.

"There are a couple of inviolate principles in the universe," I said, suddenly chatty (I was delighted to be where we were). "One is that you never get *anything worth getting* from an asshole. Two is when a stranger comes toward you with his hand extended, he doesn't want to be your friend. Are you with me?"

As if a thirsty genie had joined us, the beers vanished in their bottles. "Maybe we should go again?" I said. I held up two fingers for the waiter and swirled them around in the soupy air. He came over.

"How do you keep them so cold?" I asked. I was having a good time.

"*¿Qué?*"

"It's okay, *no importa.*"

A bird twittered in a nearby tree.

"First one of the day," I said. I looked over at Jesse. "Everything okay with Claire Brinkman?" He sat forward, his face darkened. "None of my business," I said mildly. "Just chatting."

"Why?"

"She looked a little distraught when we were leaving, that's all."

He took an aggressive plug of his beer. For a second I saw in that gesture how he drank when he drank with his friends. "Can I talk to you frankly, Dad?"

"Within reason. Nothing gross."

"Claire's a little bit on the weird side." Something cold, something not so nice crept into his face like a rat in a new house.

"You want to go a little gently with Claire. She hasn't had an easy time of it." Her father, a sculptor I'd known in high school, had hanged himself with a clothesline a few years before. He was a drunk, a bullshitter, an asshole, to boot. Just the kind of guy who would off himself without the slightest thought for his kids, how they were going to take it.

"I know that story," Jesse said.

"Then tread softly."

Another bird started up, this one behind the cathedral.

"I just don't like her that much. I should but I don't."

"Are you guilty about something, Jesse? You look like you just stole your grandmother's necklace."

"No."

"It's not fair to be mad at Claire because you don't like her more. Although I understand the temptation."

"Have you ever felt it?"

"It's disappointment."

I thought it might end there but it was as if there were a thin wire extending from him at that moment, that needed a tug so the rest—whatever it was—could come out. Which silence seemed to serve.

By now the sky had turned a dark, rich blue, a red bar running across the horizon. Such extraordinary beauty, I thought, all over the world. Is it, I had to wonder, because there was a God or was it simply how millions and millions and millions of years of absolute randomness looked? Or is this simply the stuff you think about when you're happy at four o'clock in the morning?

I called over the waiter. "Do you have any cigars?"

"*Sí, señor.*" His voice echoed in the empty square. He produced a pair from a jar on the counter and brought them over. Ten bucks each. But where else would you get a cigar at this time of the morning?

"I've been phoning another girl," Jesse said.

"Oh." I bit off the end of a cigar and handed it to him. "Who?"

He said a name I didn't recognize. He looks furtive, dishonest, I thought.

"Just a couple of times," he said.

"Uh-huh."

Puff, puff. Face averted. "I'm too young to settle on one person, don't you think?"

"That's not really the point, is it?"

A moment later we heard a soft strumming. A young man sat slumped over a guitar on the cathedral steps, slowly running his fingers over the strings. In the blue morning light he reminded me of a Picasso painting.

"Do you believe that?" Jesse said. "Have you ever seen anything so"—he looked for the word—"so perfect."

We smoked our cigars in silence for a moment, the chords hanging in the soft summer air.

"Dad?" he said suddenly.

"Yes."

"It's Rebecca I've been phoning."

"I see." Pause. Puff. Chirp. "Not that other person you mentioned."

"I didn't want you to think I was a loser. That I was obsessed with Rebecca Ng."

The sky softened to a lighter blue; the moon fading; strum, strum. "Am I obsessed with Rebecca?" he asked.

"Nothing wrong with being obsessed with a woman, Jesse."

"Have you ever been?"

"Please," I said, "don't let me commence."

"I haven't told my mom. She'll start crying and talking about Claire's feelings. Are you surprised?"

"About Rebecca? No. I always thought you had a second act there."

"Do you think so? Is that right?" The idea excited him and I felt a sudden pang of dread, as if I were watching him drive a slowly accelerating car toward a cement wall.

"Can I just say one thing to you?"

"Sure."

"Love affairs that start in blood tend to end up in blood."

The waiter came over and collected a few chairs from the table next to us and took them inside the café.

"Jesus, Dad."

CHAPTER 5

WHEN I GOT BACK FROM CUBA, I was mildly surprised not to find a phone message from Derek H. The first shoot of the Viagra documentary was supposed to start in a month; we had no final script. I waited a day, then another and sent him a jolly e-mail. (I loathed its tone of phony camaraderie.) His answer came almost immediately. He had been offered a two-hour documentary on Nelson Mandela: full interview access to him, to his ex-wife, even some of his cronies from prison. There was a time factor at play—Mandela was eighty-six years old; surely I could understand. He was, Derek concluded, terrible sorry, but he had just "run out of time."

I was floored. Not to mention broke after the "celebratory" trip to Cuba. I also felt that I'd been had. Lured into a frivolous, undignified piece of work that made me look like a fool. I remembered my words to Jesse in the cathedral square, the missionary's zeal with which I'd delivered them. "You never get *anything worth getting* from an asshole."

I stomped up and down the living room with my fists clenched and swearing revenge; Jesse listened quietly, numb with guilt, I imagine. I went to bed drunk; woke up at four in the morning to pee; just as I flushed the toilet, my watch slipped from my wrist and whirled down the chute. I sat down on the toilet seat and slid quietly into tears. Here I'd let Jesse drop out of school, I'd promised to look after him, and now it turned out I couldn't even look after myself. A bullshitter, just like Claire Brinkman's father.

By morning, I could feel a kind of terror spread through my chest like poison. My heart raced; it was as if a belt were slowly tightening around me. Finally I couldn't stand it anymore. Just to do something, to move, I climbed onto my bicycle and rode downtown. It was a funereal summer day, muggy and full of unattractive people. I was walking my bike through a narrow alleyway when I noticed a bicycle courier riding cautiously my way. He was wearing sunglasses, a big bag thrown over his shoulder, gloves without fingers. But what interested me about him was that he appeared to be my age. "Excuse me," I said. "You're a courier, yes?"

"Yes."

I asked him if he had time for a few questions. How much did he make? About $120 a day. A *day*? Yep, if he hustled. I asked who he worked for, he named the company. He was an easygoing fellow with perfect white teeth.

"Do you think it might be possible for me to get a job with your company?" I asked.

He raised his sunglasses and looked at me with his clear blue eyes. "Aren't you the guy from television?"

"Not at this moment."

He said, "I used to watch you all the time. I saw you interview Michael Moore. What a prick that guy is."

I said, "So what do you think?"

He looked down the alleyway and frowned. He said, "Well, we have an age limit. You've got to be under fifty."

I said, "Are you under fifty?"

"No, but I've been there a long time."

I said, "Could you do me a favor? Could you speak to your boss on my behalf? Tell him I'm not fooling around here—I'll stay for at least six months, I'm in good shape."

He hesitated. "That's going to be a pretty weird conversation."

I wrote down my name and phone number and gave it to him.

"I'd be really grateful," I said.

A day went by, then a few days, then nothing; I never heard back from him.

"Can you believe this?" I said to Tina. "I can't even get a job as a fucking bike courier."

In the middle of a silent breakfast the following morning, I rose from my chair and went back to bed, fully clothed. I put my head under the covers and tried to get back to sleep. A few moments later I felt a presence like a small bird alight on the side of the bed.

"I can help you with this," Tina said, "but you have to let me. You can't fight with me."

An hour later she gave me a list of twenty names.

Newspaper editors, cable television producers, people in public relations, speechwriters, even a local politician we vaguely knew. She said, "You have to call these people and tell them you're available for work."

"I already have."

"No, you haven't. You just looked up your old pals. "

I looked at the first name on the list. "Not that fuckweed. I can't call *him*!"

She shushed me. "You said you wouldn't fight about this."

So I didn't. I gave myself a day's respite and then I sat down at the kitchen table and started making my calls. And to my surprise, she was right. Most everybody was pretty decent. They didn't have anything for me at the moment, but they were friendly, encouraging.

In a moment of energized optimism (phoning is better than waiting), I said to Jesse, "This is my problem, not yours." But he wasn't a lout or a parasite and I could feel him tiptoeing around "the situation," could feel him almost wince when he asked for ten dollars for this, ten dollars for that. But what could he do? He didn't have a bean. His mother was helping out but she was an actor, a stage actor at that. And it certainly wasn't up to Tina to crack into her savings (started when she was sixteen) to support my son, whose free-floating, it'll-happen-dude posture I had so confidently encouraged. In the middle of the night (when little good comes from thinking about anything), I wondered how unpleasant things were going to get, how toxic the atmosphere around money, if my luck didn't change soon.

The film club resumed. To lure Jesse into watching more movies without making it too school-like, I made up a game of spot-the-great-moment. This meant a scene or a bit of dialogue or image that snaps you forward in your seat, makes your heart bang. We started with an easy one, Stanley Kubrick's *The Shining* (1980), the story of a failed writer (Jack Nicholson) who goes slowly mad in a deserted hotel and tries to murder his family.

The Shining is probably director Stanley Kubrick's best film. But Stephen King, the author of the novel, loathed the movie and disliked Kubrick. A lot of people did; Kubrick was famous for being a finicky, self-adoring man who made actors do things over and over with questionable results; when filming the scene where Jack Nicholson ambushes Scatman Crothers with an ax, Kubrick made them do it forty times; finally, seeing that the seventy-year-old Crothers was visibly exhausted, Nicholson told Kubrick that was enough takes—he wasn't going to do it again.

Later on in the filming Jack pursued his knife-wielding wife (Shelley Duvall) up the stairs fifty-eight times before Kubrick was happy. (Was it worth the work? Could the second or third take have done as well? Probably.)

But more important, Stephen King felt that Kubrick just "didn't get it" when it came to horror, didn't have a clue how it worked. King went to an early screening of *The Shining* and came away disgusted; he said the movie was like a Cadillac without an engine. "You get in, you can smell the leather, but you can't drive it anywhere." In fact, he went on to say he thought Kubrick made movies to "hurt people."

Which I sort of agree with, but I love *The Shining*; I love the way it's shot and lit, I love the sound of the tricycle wheels going from carpet to wood to carpet. It always scares me when the twin girls appear in the hallway. For my great moment, though, I picked the scene where Jack Nicholson hallucinates a conversation between himself and a hotel waiter, a stiff British-butler type. It takes places in an almost blindingly lit washroom—electric orange and white. The dialogue begins innocently enough but then the waiter warns Jack that his young son is "making trouble," that maybe he should be "dealt with." The waiter (Philip Stone) steals the scene with his precise stillness and quiet line readings; watch the way he closes his dry lips at the end of each phrase. It's like a delicate, vaguely obscene punctuation mark.

He had problems with his own children, the waiter confides. One of them didn't like the hotel and tried to burn it down. But he "corrected" her (with an ax). "And when my wife tried to prevent me from doing my duty, I 'corrected' her." It's a letter-perfect performance. Unlike Jack's, which has not aged so well since I first saw it in 1980. Here he seems hammy, almost amateurish, surprisingly bad, especially alongside this exquisitely controlled English actor.

That wasn't Jesse's great moment, though; he chose the scene where the little boy steals into Jack's bedroom early in the morning to retrieve a toy, only to find his father sitting on the side of the bed with the thousand-yard stare. Jack summons over his son, who sits uneasily on his lap. Looking at his father's unshaven face and bleary eyes—in a blue dressing gown Nicholson's as pale as a corpse—the little boy asks him why he doesn't go to sleep.

After a beat comes the chilling response: "I've got too

much to do." Meaning, we intuit, chop up his family just like the waiter did.

"That's it, " Jesse whispered. "Can we play it again?"

We watched *Annie Hall* (1977) for, among other reasons, the scene where Diane Keaton sings "Seems Like Old Times" in a dark bar. Keaton is shot slightly from the side and appears to be looking at someone off camera. It's a scene that gives me goose bumps—she seems to be singing the song, making its dramatic points, with her eyes. It's also a moment of self-realization, for her character, Annie Hall, a fledgling musician, is taking apprehensive but certain first flight.

Some films let you down; you must have been in love or heartbroken, you must have been wound up about something when you saw them, because now, viewed from a different trajectory, there's no magic left. I showed him *Around the World in 80 Days* (1956) which, with its glorious shot of a balloon floating over Paris at sunset, had knocked me out when I was his age but now seemed appallingly dated and silly.

But some films still do it, still give you a thrill years and years later. I showed Jesse *Mean Streets* (1973), a movie that Martin Scorsese made at the very beginning of his career. It's about growing up in New York's violent, macho Little Italy. There's a sequence near the beginning I've never forgotten. With the dramatic chords of the Rolling Stones' "Tell Me" in the background, the camera follows Harvey Keitel in his passage through a red-lit bar. Anyone who has gone into a favorite bar on a Friday night knows that moment. You know everyone, they wave, they call out your name, the whole night is before you. Keitel snakes his way through the crowd, shaking hands here, exchanging a joke there; he's dancing slowly, just in the hip, to the music; it's a portrait of a young man in love with life, in love with being alive on this Friday night with these people in this place. It also bears the signature of a young filmmaker's joy, a moment of transport, when he's doing it, he's actually *making a movie*.

There were other great moments: Gene Hackman rousting a bar in *The French Connection* (1971). "Popeye's here!" he cries, rushing down the counter, pill bottles, switchblades, joints hitting the floor. There's Charles Grodin's double-take in *Ishtar* (1987) when Dustin Hoffman asks him if Libya is "near here." Or Marlon Brando's monologue in *Last Tango in Paris* (1972) about a dog named Dutchie who used to "jump up and look around for rabbits" in a mustard field. We watched *Last Tango* late at night, a candle burning on the table, and at the end of the scene I could see Jesse's dark eyes staring over at me.

"Yep," I said.

There's Audrey Hepburn on the fire escape of a brownstone Manhattan apartment in *Breakfast at Tiffany's* (1961), her hair wrapped in an after-shower towel, her fingers gently strumming a guitar. The camera takes it all in, the stairwell, the bricks, the slim woman, then changes to a medium-tight shot, just Audrey; then blam, a full close-up, her face fills the screen, those porcelain cheekbones, the sharp chin, the brown eyes. She stops strumming and looks up, surprised, at somebody off camera. "Hi," she says softly. That's one of those moments people go to movies for; you see it once, no matter at what age, you never forget it. It is an example of what films can do, how they can slip past your defenses and really break your heart.

I sat smitten as the credits rolled, the theme song fading, but I sensed a reserve on Jesse's part as if he were reluctant to walk across a carpet in muddy shoes, so to speak.

"What?" I said.

"It's a peculiar movie," he said, suppressing a yawn, something he sometimes did when he was uncomfortable.

"How so?"

"It's about a pair of prostitutes. But the movie itself doesn't seem to know that. It seems to think it's about something sort of sweet and nutty." Here he laughed. "I don't mean to be disrespectful about something you really like—"

"No, no," I said defensively. "I don't really like it. I like *her*." I went on to say that Truman Capote, who wrote the novella the movie was based on, never liked the casting of Audrey Hepburn. "He thought Holly Golightly was more of a tomboy, more of a Jodie Foster type."

"For sure," Jesse said. "You just can't imagine Audrey Hepburn as a hooker. And the woman in that movie is a hooker. So is the guy, the young writer. They both do it for money."

Holly Golightly a hooker?

———

Jesse asked me once, did I think Rebecca was out of his league? I said no, but I had private worries—that the competition for such a stunning creature, particularly the *arena* in which it might be played out (stylish superficialities), might defeat him. I remember him turning his pale, despairing face to me in those weeks after "the incident" and saying,

"I think God is going to give me everything I want in life except Rebecca Ng."

So once he "got" her, I was relieved—because it meant that for the next while at least, he wouldn't be haunted by the suspicion that a higher happiness lay just beyond his fingertips. Thinking back on it, I imagine it was the cafeteria rumors about Claire Brinkman that revived Rebecca's interest in him—in old "huggable" Jesse. Rumors that blew her nerdy boyfriend far out to sea and, sadly, took Claire with them.

The truth is, though, once you got past her dazzling looks, Rebecca Ng was a weapons-grade pain in the ass. She was a stirrer of the pot, a lover of intrigue and distress, a creature who seemed to draw oxygen from the spectacle of people at each other's throat, everybody in a state of upset and talking about *her*. It put color in those sunken, movie-star cheeks.

She'd telephone Jesse late at night and imply disturbing things. She was having second thoughts. Maybe they should "date" other people and see if it was "a good fit." All this reserved for the final seconds of the call. It was her way of keeping him on the line. She couldn't stand for him to be the one to say, "I have to go now. Good-bye."

Hours and hours went by like this, conversations that left him ragged and feeling as if there were sand in his eyes. I worried she was going to scar him.

But there was a small *unhavable* part in Jesse, something all the other boys gave her that he, for reasons I still don't understand, withheld, a single, dark room in the mansion to which Rebecca had no access, and it obsessed her. You knew the moment she got in there with a flashlight, the moment

she understood she could come and go, it would be a valueless room, *he* would be valueless, and she'd move on. But for
the moment it was a locked door and she waited outside,
trying to find the key that would turn the bolt.

On warm afternoons, birds chirping, lawn mowers buzzing, hammers banging on the converted church across the
street, Rebecca Ng appeared on our porch, her black hair
gleaming with health and vitality. For two or three minutes,
she engaged me in breezy, impersonal conversation, the kind
you expect from a politician at a fundraiser. Chat, chat, chat.
Fearless eye contact. The kind of girl who was going to run
a string of world-class hotels one day.

Duty done, she descended into the basement. The door
at the foot of the stairs closed with a soft, firm click. I heard
the murmur of young voices and then, wondering if I should
remind Jesse to brush his teeth or put a pillow slip on the
pillow (and deciding not to), I removed myself to a distant,
soundproof part of the house.

How perfect, I thought, that "straight-A" Rebecca Ng
should be having a fully realized love affair with a high
school dropout. Wasn't that just what her parents had in
mind when they fled Vietnam in a rowboat?

On those other afternoons when she was overachieving at
a manager-in-training course or preparing a debate with the
Young Conservatives Caucus, Jesse and I watched movies
on the couch. I can see from my yellow cards that we spent
a couple of weeks on a "unit" (there's a despicable "school"
word) called Talent Will Out. This was simply a small group
of films, sometimes not very good, where an unknown actor
turns in a performance so good that, to put it vulgarly, you

know it's only a question of time before he or she becomes a huge movie star. Think of Samuel L. Jackson as a crackhead in Spike Lee's *Jungle Fever* (1991). You watch it for thirty seconds: "Who is *that* guy?" Or Winona Ryder's tiny role in *Beetlejuice* (1988).

Same thing, of course, for Sean Penn's performance as a stoner in the high school sex comedy *Fast Times at Ridgemont High* (1982). Watch the way he looks at people when they're talking to him. It's as if he is deafened by the sound of white noise in his head and has a pillow squeezed between his ears. It's not a leading role, but Penn stands so solidly in the middle of the film, his talent so authentic, so glaring, that everyone is reduced to a kind of backup singer (the same "graying" effect that Gary Cooper had on his fellow actors).

"Do *I* have talent?" Jesse asked.

"Tons," I said.

"That kind of talent?"

What do you say? "The trick," I said, "to having a happy life is being good at something. Do you suspect that you might be good at something?"

"I don't know what."

I told him about André Gide, the French novelist, who wrote in his diary that it enraged him when, at the age of twenty, he walked down a Paris street and people couldn't tell just by looking in his eyes the masterpieces he would produce.

Jesse sat forward in his seat. "That's *exactly* how I feel," he said.

I showed him Audrey Hepburn in *Roman Holiday* (1953). It was her first film as a lead; she was twenty-four and inexperienced, but her easy, comedic timing with Gregory Peck seemed to spring from an inexplicable artistic maturity. How did she get so good so fast? And with that strange accent and a kind of emotional keenness, she is oddly reminiscent of Tolstoy's romantic heroine Natasha. But Ms. Hepburn also had that thing you can't learn, an intuitive rapport with the camera, one successful, attractive gesture after another.

I asked Jesse to again watch what happens when the camera settles on her face; it feels as if it has come to rest where it rightly belongs, as though drawn by gravity. *Roman Holiday* won her an Academy Award.

I picked the debut of a young director as part of our Talent Will Out program. To this day, this largely forgotten little TV movie remains one of the most exhilarating pieces of youthful, look-at-me filmmaking I've ever seen.

Movies for television tend not to be the domain of the brilliant, but seconds into *Duel* (1971), you can tell that something odd is going on. You see, from the driver's point of view, a car leaving the pleasant suburbs of some American city and heading slowly out of town. It's a hot day, blue sky; houses thin out, traffic thins out, the car is alone.

Then, out of nowhere, a rusted eighteen-wheel transport truck appears in the rearview mirror. Its windows are shaded. You never see the driver. You glimpse his cowboy boots, his hand waving out the window, but never his face.

For seventy-four minutes, like a prehistoric monster, the truck chases the car through the sun-baked landscape. It is Moby Dick seeking out Ahab. Waiting by the roadside, hiding in gulleys, appearing to lose interest then suddenly reappearing, the truck is a vector of irrational evil; it is the hand under the bed waiting to grab your ankle. But why? (Hint: Even at his young age, the director knew not to answer the question.)

A truck and a car—no dialogue between them. Just running down the highway. How, I asked Jesse, could anyone animate such material? "Like squeezing wine from a rock," he said.

I suggested that the answer lay in the director's visual attack. *Duel* compels you to look at it. It seems to say to the audience, There is something of primordial importance going on here; you have feared this very thing *before* and now here it is again.

Steven Spielberg was twenty-four when he directed *Duel*. He'd done some television (a *Columbo* episode served as his calling card) but no one anticipated that he was going to tear up the material with quite this relish. More than the truck, more than Dennis Weaver's escalatingly frightened driver, the director is the star of *Duel*. Like reading the first pages of a great novel, you sense you're in the presence of an enormous, *incautious* talent. It hasn't learned to second-guess itself, to be too smart. Which is what, I suppose, Spielberg meant a few years ago when he told an interviewer that he tried to rewatch *Duel* every two or three years in order to "remember how I did it." You have to be young, he implied, to be so unapologetically sure-footed.

You can see why studio executives took one look at *Duel* and gave him *Jaws* (1975) a few years later. If Spielberg could make an unwieldy truck scary, just imagine what he could do with a shark (which, like the driver of the truck, remains largely out of sight. You see only its effects, a missing dog, a girl pulled suddenly underwater, a buoy exploding to the surface, things that announce the presence of danger but never give it a face. Spielberg intuited at an early age that if you want to scare people, let their imaginations do the heavy lifting).

We watched "The Making of *Duel*," which came with the DVD. To my surprise, Jesse was intrigued listening to Spielberg talk about the shot-by-shot construction of the movie—how much thought had gone into it, how much work. The storyboards, the multiple cameras, even auditioning a half-dozen trucks to see which looked the meanest. "You know, Dad," he said in a tone of mild amazement, "up till now, I've always thought Spielberg was a bit of a suck."

"He's a film nerd," I said. "Slightly different species." I told him the story about a young, hard-partying actress who knew Spielberg and George Lucas and Brian De Palma and Martin Scorsese in California when they were just starting out. She was amazed, she later said, that they didn't seem to be interested in girls or drugs. All they wanted to do was hang around with one another and talk about movies. "Like I said, nerds."

I showed him *A Streetcar Named Desire* (1951). I told him how in 1948, a young, relatively unknown actor, Marlon Brando, hitchhiked from New York to Tennessee Williams's house in Provincetown, Massachusetts, to audition for the Broadway production, how he found the celebrated playwright in a state of terrible anxiety; the electricity was out and the toilets were stopped up. There was no water. Brando fixed the power problem by putting pennies behind the fuses and then got down on his hands and knees and fixed the plumbing; when that was done, he dried his hands and went into the living room to read the part of Stanley Kowalski. He read for maybe thirty seconds, so the story goes, before Tennessee, who was half bombed, waved him to silence and said, "That's fine," and sent him back to New York with the part.

And his performance? There were actors who quit acting when they saw Brando do *Streetcar* on Broadway in 1949. (The same way Virginia Woolf wanted to give it up when she first read Proust.) But the studio didn't want Brando for the film. He was too young. He mumbled. But his acting teacher Stella Adler had made the ominous prediction early on that this "strange puppy thing" was going to be the greatest actor of his generation. Which is how it turned out.

Years later, students who took acting workshops with Brando remembered his unorthodox ways, how he could recite a Shakespearean monologue standing on his head and still make it truer, more affecting, than anyone else's work that day.

"*Streetcar*," I explained, "was the play where they let the genie out of the bottle; it literally changed the whole style of American acting."

"You could feel it," Karl Malden, who played Mitch in the original Broadway production, said years later. "The audience wanted Brando; they came for Brando; and when he was offstage, you could *feel* them waiting for him to come back."

I realized I was getting dangerously close to overselling the film so I forced myself to stop talking. "Okay," I said to

Jesse, "you are really going to see something today. Buckle up."

Sometimes the phone rang; I dreaded that. If it was Rebecca Ng, the mood would be shattered as certainly as if a vandal had thrown a rock through the window. One afternoon, a honey-hot day in late August, Jesse disappeared to take a call in the middle of *Some Like It Hot* (1959); he was gone twenty minutes, returning distracted and unhappy. I put the movie back on but I was acutely aware of his absent attention. He had settled his eyes on the television screen as a kind of anchor so that his worried thoughts about Rebecca might roam freely.

I snapped off the DVD. I said, "You know, Jesse, these movies were put together with a great deal of thought and love. They were meant to be watched in one sitting, one scene flowing out of another. So I'm going to make a rule here. From now on, no phone calls during the movie. It's disrespectful and it's shitty."

"Okay," he said.

"We don't even look at the number when it comes up, okay?"

"Okay, okay."

The phone rang again. (Even from across the city, Rebecca seemed to sense when his attention was elsewhere.)

"You better take it. This time anyway."

"I'm with my dad," he whispered. "I'll call you back." A buzz like a small hornet trapped inside the earpiece. "I'm with my dad," he repeated.

He put down the phone.

"What is it?" I said.

"Nothing." Then with an exasperated exhalation, as if he had been holding his breath, he said, "Rebecca always picks the strangest times to want to talk about stuff." For an instant I thought I saw tears misting up in his eyes.

"What stuff?"

"Our relationship."

We went back to the movie but I sensed he wasn't there anymore. He was watching some other movie, the bad things Rebecca was going to do because he'd pissed her off on the phone. I turned off the television. He looked at me, startled, as if he might be in trouble.

"I had a girlfriend once," I said. "All we ever talked about was our relationship. That's what we did instead of having one. It gets to be a real bore. Call her back. Clear it up."

CHAPTER

ONE MORNING, AFTER A HEAT WAVE that had lasted nearly a week, the air was suddenly different. There was dew on the car hoods; the clouds seemed unnaturally vivid in their procession across the sky. Autumn, not tomorrow or even the next week, was irreversibly on its way. I was taking a shortcut through the Manulife building on Bloor Street when I spotted Paul Bouissac sitting alone in the café beside the escalator. He was a short, owl-faced Frenchman who had taught me a university course in surrealism thirty years before and who had maintained a mildly insulting commentary on my career in television ever since. It was beneath him to watch me, he implied, but his boyfriend, a damp-handed nightmare, was a great fan. (Which I rather doubted, but never mind.)

Bouissac raised a plump, white hand and waved me over. Obediently I sat down. We talked about this and that, I asking the questions (*comme d'habitude*), he shrugging at their naïve provenance. This was the way we conversed. When the subject of Jesse arose ("*Et vous, vous tuez la journée comment?*"), I launched into my spiel, how a distaste for school was "hardly a pathology," perhaps even "*quelque chose d'encourageant*," how I was dealing with a kid who didn't watch TV or do drugs. That happy children go on to have happy lives, etc., etc., etc. I went on a bit, and while I spoke, I found myself experiencing a strange shortness of breath, as if I had just run up a flight of stairs. Bouissac waved me to silence and I could feel my little car, so to speak, pull to the sidewalk with an ungraceful lurch.

"You are being defensive," he said in heavily accented English. (Forty years in Toronto and still sounding like Charles de Gaulle.) I insisted I wasn't and then grew more so. Explained things that didn't require explaining, defended myself against criticisms that had not been leveled.

"There is a period for learning. After that it is too late," said Bouissac with the intolerable finality of the French intellectual.

Too late? Does he mean, I wondered, that learning is like the mastery of a language, you have to "get" the accent before a certain age (twelve or thirteen) or you never get it right? Distressing thought. Should we have sent him to a military school?

Losing interest (and showing it), Bouissac finished off his tiny espresso, and wandered off in search of a pair of new oven mitts. He was hosting a dinner party for a clutch of international semioticians that very night. The encounter left me surprisingly jarred. I felt as though I'd betrayed something, had sold myself short. Was I being defensive about Jesse or about myself? Was I boasting like a ten-year-old in the schoolyard? Was it that transparent? Perhaps so. But I didn't want anyone to think I was doing Jesse a bad turn. (I couldn't shake that image of him piloting a marijuana-clouded cab.)

Three teenage girls swished by, smelling of gum and cold air. Perhaps, I thought, the influence we have over our children is an overrated thing. How exactly do you force a six-foot-four teenager to do homework assignments? No, we had already lost that one, his mother and I.

A dislike for Bouissac, like a sudden, unexpected gust of wind, passed over me and I had a feeling that down the road this curious student-like behavior of mine, this habitual deference, was going to undergo a rather nasty metamorphosis.

Right there at the table, I got out a pen and made a list on a napkin of all the young men I'd gone to university with who hadn't amounted to a hill of beans. There was B., who drank himself to death in Mexico; G., my boyhood best friend, who shot a man in the face with a shotgun while in a drugged stupor; M., a whiz kid at math, at sports, at everything, whose days were now spent masturbating in front of his computer while his wife worked in a downtown law firm. It was a comforting, dramatic list. There was even my brother, my sad, sad brother—track star, frat king in university, who now lived in the corner room of a boardinghouse, still railing, even after all these years, about the iniquities of his education.

But what if I was wrong? What if Jesse didn't come charging out of the basement one of these days and "grab the world by the lapels"? What if I'd allowed him to fuck up his entire life under some misinformed theory that might just be laziness with a smart-ass spin on it? Again, I saw a taxi driving slowly down University Avenue on a rain-slicked night. The graveyard shift. Jesse, a guy they know in the all-night doughnut store. "Hey, Jess. The usual? That should do her."

Had he learned *anything* over the last year under my "tutelage"? Was any of it worth knowing? Let's see. He knew about Elia Kazan and the House Un-American thing, but did he know what communists were? He knew that Vittorio Storaro lit the apartment in *Last Tango in Paris* by putting the lights on the *outside* of the windows rather than inside on the set, but did he know where Paris was? He knew that you left your fork facedown until your meal was over, that French cabernets tended to be slightly more sour than California cabs. (Important stuff.) What else? To eat with your mouth closed (patchy), to brush your tongue as well as your teeth in the morning (catching hold). To rinse the tuna juice from the side of the sink when you're finished making your sandwich (almost).

Oh, but listen. He loved Gary Oldman's psychotic charge down the hall with a shotgun in *The Professional* (1994). He loved Marlon Brando sweeping the dishes off the dining room table in *A Streetcar Named Desire*. "My place is cleared. You want me to clear your places?" He loved *Swimming with Sharks* (1994), not the early moments ("That's just shtick") but the end part. ("That," he said, "is where it gets quite profound!") He loved Al Pacino in *Scarface* (1983). He loved that movie like I loved the parties in *The Great Gatsby*. You know they're naughty and shallow but you want to go to them anyway. He watched *Annie Hall* over and over. I would find the empty DVD case on the couch in the morning. He knew it almost line by line, could quote from it. Ditto with *Hannah and Her Sisters* (1986). He was knocked cold by Adrian Lyne's *Lolita* (1997). He wanted it for Christmas. Were these things I should feel happy about?

Yes, in fact.

But then one day, snow falling outside the living room window, we were watching a replay of *Scarface*, the scene where Al arrives in Miami, when Jesse turned and asked me where Florida was.

"Huh?"

He said, "From here. How do you get to it from here?"

After a judicious pause (Was he joking?), I said, "You go south."

"Toward Eglinton or toward King Street?"

"King Street."

"Yeah?"

I proceeded carefully but respectfully in the tones of one who might at any second be ambushed by a practical joke. But this was no joke. "You go down to King Street and you keep going till you get to the lake; you cross over the lake and that's the beginning of the States." I waited for him to stop me.

"The United States is right across the lake?" he said.

"Uh-huh." Pause. "You keep going down through the States, maybe fifteen hundred miles, Pennsylvania, the Carolinas, Georgia"—still waiting for him to stop me—"until you get to a finger-shaped state that sticks out into the water. That's Florida."

"Oh." Pause. "What's after that?"

"After Florida?"

"Yeah."

"Well, let's see. You go right to the bottom of the finger until you hit another patch of water; you keep going another hundred miles, you hit Cuba. Remember Cuba? That's where we had that long conversation about Rebecca."

"That was a great conversation."

"Stay with me," I said. "You go past Cuba, a long way past, until you get to South America."

"Is that a country?"

Pause. "No, that's a continent. You keep on going, thousands and thousands of miles, jungles and cities, jungles and cities, all the way down to the end of Argentina."

He stared into space. He was seeing something very vivid in his imagination, but God knows what it was.

"Is that the end of the world?" he asked.

"Pretty much."

Am I doing the right thing here?

———————————

It was spring now on Maggie's street. The trees, budding at their very tips like fingernails, appeared to be extending their branches toward the sun. It was in the course of showing one of those highfalutin art movies that something very odd happened, a perfect illustration of the very lesson the movie was trying to teach. It started when I heard the house next door was for sale. Not our through-the-wall neighbor, Eleanor—the only way she was leaving her place was feet first with a Union Jack clamped to her forehead—but the couple on the other side, the snake-slim woman in the sunglasses and her bald husband.

Entirely by coincidence I picked that week to show Jesse the Italian classic *The Bicycle Thief* (1948). Just the saddest story ever. An unemployed guy needs a bike for a job, gets one with great difficulty; his whole demeanor changes, his sexual confidence returns. But the bike gets stolen the next day. He's in agony. The actor, Lamberto Maggiorani, has the face of an inarticulate, devastated child. What's he to do? No bike, no job. It's almost too upsetting to watch as he runs all over town with his son looking for the lost vehicle. Then he spots an unguarded bicycle and steals it. In other words, he chooses to inflict the same agony on somebody else that has been visited upon him. It's for his family's welfare, he rationalizes—it's not like the other guy. The point being, I explain, that we sometimes calibrate our moral positions, what's right, what's wrong, depending on what we need at that particular moment. Jesse nods; the idea engages him. You can see him rumbling about in the incidents of his own life, stopping here and there, looking for a parallel.

But the bicycle thief gets caught, and caught publicly. It's as if the whole neighborhood turns out to see him hauled away. Including his son, on whose face is an expression none of us ever want to see on our children's faces.

The day after the screening, maybe a few days later, there were comings and goings next door; I saw a skinny, rat-faced fellow nosing around in the alleyway among my new garbage cans. Then one morning, the city looking gray in a sort of fortified way, puddles and litter in the streets as if the tide had gone out (you almost expected to see a dying fish flapping in the gutters), a FOR SALE sign appeared.

I found myself wondering, idly at first, then with increasing momentum, if I should sell my bachelor loft in the candy factory (it had appreciated wildly) and move in next door to my son and my beloved ex-wife. Provided they wanted me, of course. The more I thought about it, the more I wanted to do it, the more urgent it seemed. In a matter of days, the question assumed almost lifesaving significance. I might even, I concluded, have a little living money left over from the down payment. This wasn't how I'd thought my life would go but I'd had worse ideas. Maybe it would change my luck, just living near the two of them. Late one afternoon, my sexy neighbor in sunglasses pulled to the corner in her small, utilitarian car and hurried up the steps, briefcase in hand.

"I hear you're selling your house," I said.

"That's right," she said, not missing a beat, slipping the key into the lock.

"Any chance I could have an advance peek?"

You could see that rat-faced real estate agent had warned her against doing exactly this. But she was a decent soul and said, "Sure."

It was a little man's house, a Frenchman's house, but clean and welcoming, even in the recesses of the basement (unlike Maggie's basement, where, just past the washing machine, one feared a crocodile attack). Narrow hallways, narrow stairs, meticulously painted bedrooms, detailed border work, and a bathroom medicine cabinet that prompted curiosity—although given her clear complexion, her aura of constant and purposeful motion, she didn't seem the kind to have any pills worth pinching.

"How much?" I asked.

She named a figure. It was absurdly high, naturally, but then so was the recent appraisal of my candy-factory loft, which had, so I was told, "come into fashion" with a whole species of obnoxious young success stories (cell phone, three-day beard). A place for winners, for swingers. For assholes, in a word.

I explained my situation: I passionately wanted to live near my teenage son and my ex-wife. That took her aback. Could she let me have first crack at buying the house? Yes, she said. She'd talk to her husband.

There was quite the flurry of activity at our house. Calls to the bank, to Maggie at the loft (a delighted green light accompanied by moist eyes), another chat with Slim next door. Everything looking good.

But then, for reasons I couldn't fathom, Slim and her egghead husband decided not to offer us first anything. There would be two showings, he informed me stiffly one evening, after which we were welcome to make a bid. Along with everyone else. Not good news. Greektown was coming into vogue as well; the prices were terrifying. Houses were getting $200,000 more than the asking price.

A day or two before "show day," I took Jesse aside. I asked him to round up a bunch of his buddies for an afternoon on the porch. Beer and cigarettes on me. Starting time, exactly 2:00 P.M.

You can imagine the spectacle. As potential buyers fluttered up the stairs next door, they passed a half-dozen drinking, smoking, toque-wearing "louts" in sunglasses and pale complexions on the adjacent porch. Their new "neighbors," three feet away. Some cars stopped, paused for an inspection, two moons frozen in the passenger window, and then moved away.

After an hour or so, the rat-faced real estate agent emerged and asked the lads if the owner was home. I was cringing in the living room, trying to watch television, my entrails shuddering as if a car alarm were going off inside me. (Guilty conscience.)

"No, no," I whispered to Jesse, "tell him I'm not here."

At four o'clock the showing ended. Twenty minutes later, as I was stealing down the front stairs to get a drink at the local Greek restaurant, my nerves shot, the agent appeared. He had a small, bony face as if unpleasant judgments had shrunk the skin and given it an off-putting shine. The "gentlemen on the porch," he said, were posing "quite the problem." I tried to change the subject; in jolly tones I asked him about the real estate business, about the neighborhood; maybe I'd use him myself—I was going to buy a house. Ha, ha, ha, my pirate's laugh. He was not put off. Unsmiling, he said they'd frightened off a number of buyers with their swearing. Never! I said, as if defending my queen.

There was a showing the following day, Sunday. A fine rain fell, the sky a soft gray, seagulls flying low over the park, some walking with their heads back, their beaks open, as if they were gargling. In spite of profound misgivings, I persisted in my strategy. More beer, more cigarettes, more hunched-over louts glaring into the middle distance. I didn't have the stomach to stick around and beetled off across the bridge on my bicycle to take care of some imaginary business. I didn't come back until after four. The rain had let up. I was just passing the Greek restaurant where we often ate when I saw Jesse walking along the sidewalk toward me. He was smiling but there was something cautious, almost protective about it.

"We had a little problem," he said. A few minutes into the showing, the bald man had stormed across the lawn—this time *he* was wearing the sunglasses—and knocked on the door with both fists. With the louts looking on, he demanded to see me.

Me?

"He's not here," Jesse told him.

"I know what he's doing," Baldy roared. "He's trying to *assassinate* the sale."

Assassinate the sale? Tough words. Especially since they were true. I felt a sudden, sickening wave of shame; even worse, I had the adolescent sensation, like flames licking at the inside of a house, that I was in "big trouble." That I'd taken out my dad's car without a license and cracked it up. I also had the uncomfortable feeling that Jesse knew I was in the wrong, had known it all along. Not to mention the fact that I'd implicated *him* in it. A sterling example of parental guidance. How to handle a crisis. How to get what you want. Put him in my hands, Maggie, I'll make sure he straightens up and flies right.

"I got everybody inside," he said.

"Is it safe to go back?"

"I'd wait awhile. He's pretty pissed off."

A few days later, I asked a friend of mine to "beard" for me, pretend he was the purchaser and put in a bid on the house. But they must have seen clear through it; they hardly gave him the time of day. It had all been for nothing, my machinations, my involving a bunch of kids in a stupid, unethical scheme. A gay couple with a flower shop got the house for nearly half a million dollars.

Was this episode, I wondered, going to be one of those things that Jesse remembered for the rest of his life? (You never know when the window is open. And when it is, you don't want to throw a dead dog through it.) I took him aside the next day. "That was a king-size mistake I made," I said.

"There's nothing wrong with wanting to live next door to your family," he said. But I stopped him.

I said, "If some guy did that to me when I was trying to sell *my* place, I'd go over there with a machine gun."

"I still think you did the right thing," he insisted.

It was hard to make him see things differently. I said, "I'm just like that guy in *The Bicycle Thief.* I make something the right thing to do just because I need it done."

"What if it *was* the right thing to do?" he came back.

Later, when we went outside for a postfilm cigarette, I found myself looking furtively this way and that to make sure Baldy or his wife wasn't around.

"You see the consequences?" I said. "Now I have to look out for this guy every time I go on the porch. That's the price. That's the *real* price."

CHAPTER 7

I DESIGNED A STILLNESS UNIT for us to watch. This was about how to steal a scene from all the actors around you by not moving. I started, of course, with *High Noon* (1952). There are happy accidents in the movies where everything seems to just click into place. Right script, right director, right cast. *Casablanca* (1942) is one, *The Godfather* (1972) another, and *High Noon*. A sheriff, Gary Cooper, is on his way out of town with a new bride when he hears that a very bad guy has just gotten out of jail and, along with three friends, is headed this way to "get" the man who put him away. They're coming on the noon train. Cooper runs here and there all over town trying to get help; everyone's got a good reason to say no. In the end, it's just him, an empty street, and four men with guns.

The film was made at a time when Westerns were usually in color and for the most part featured a kind of granitechinned, high-minded hero, more of a cartoon than a human being. Suddenly along came *High Noon,* shot in stark black-and-white—no pretty sunsets and gorgeous mountain ranges; what we got instead was a small, rather mean-looking town. At the center of the story was something else unusual: a man who was afraid of getting hurt and showed it.

I reminded Jesse that the film was shot in the early fifties, that you could see a parallel with the witch hunts that were going on at the same time in Hollywood. People suspected of leftist sympathies found themselves deserted by their friends overnight.

It's hardly believable now but when *High Noon* came out, it was picketed by all sorts of people. They knocked it for being anti-American. Here, they complained, was a story about a so-called hero who, at the story's end, gives up on the town's folk and leaves. The film's writer, Carl Foreman, was exiled to England; he'd been stamped a "fellow traveler," and no one would hire him. Lloyd Bridges, who plays the cowardly young hothead, didn't work again for two years; "un-American" was the verdict.

I pointed out that there are wonderful, artful things to look for in the movie. Look at the way the film shows the empty train tracks. We see them again and again. It's a wordless, eventless way of creating a sense of danger. Each time we see those tracks we are reminded that it is from that direction which evil will come. Same thing for the clocks. Tick, tick, tick, tick. They even slow down as the hour of noon approaches.

And then there is Gary Cooper. Actors who worked with him were often surprised at how little he did during a scene.

It seemed as if he hardly "acted," hardly did anything at all. But when you see his performance onscreen, it pushes everybody else into the background. Actors saw their performances disappear into a blur around him.

"Watch where your eye goes during his scenes," I told Jesse. "Imagine being a fellow actor and trying to compete with *that*."

Just so we didn't get too lofty-minded, I showed him *Internal Affairs* (1990), a nasty piece of fun, indeed. Richard Gere plays a corrupt cop. When an unstable fellow officer (William Baldwin) is called to testify, we see just how magnificent a villain Gere can create. (Better than his leading man.) With those small eyes, this is Iago on the LAPD. Gere's stillness— and the moral self-possession it suggests—is hypnotically attractive. You understand how his character holds on even to his ex-wife. And how, if he feels threatened, *nothing* is beneath him. I asked Jesse to watch for the scene where, with just a few sentences delivered in an offhand, even amused way, he cranks up the sexual horror in the imagination of Andy Garcia, the officer assigned to investigate him.

"Don't be fooled by his smug good looks, or his talk-show philosophizing," I said. "Richard Gere is the real thing."

We turned to David Cronenberg's *Dead Zone* (1983). Christopher Walken as a lonely psychic, so sad, a true prince of stillness. Then *The Godfather Part II* (1974). What can you say about "Big Al" Pacino? He has the poised, "held-in" feel of a moray eel at the mouth of a cave. Wait for that gorgeous scene with a senator who misses the significance of Pacino's second, lower offer for a casino license.

I showed *Bullitt* (1968); it came out nearly forty years ago but still has the authority of stainless steel. With a blue-eyed Steve McQueen never handsomer. McQueen was an actor who understood the value of doing very little; he listens with the titillating stillness of the great leading man. I dug up from the basement an old interview with the chatty Canadian director Norman Jewison, who made three films with McQueen.

"Steve wasn't the kind of actor who could stand onstage with a chair and entertain you," Jewison said. "He was a *movie* actor. He loved the camera and it loved him back. He was always real, partly because he was always playing himself. He never minded if you took a line away from him. Just as long as the camera was on him he was happy because he understood that it was a visual medium."

McQueen had a difficult life. He spent a couple of years in a home for delinquent boys. After a stint with the marines, he drifted to New York and took some acting classes. In other words, I explained to Jesse, this was no arty, president-of-the-drama-club guy. Talent, I said, doesn't always turn up where you think it should.

We watched *Le Samouraï* (1967) with Alain Delon, Lauren Bacall in *The Big Sleep* (1946), and, of course, the mighty Clint Eastwood (any stiller and he'd be dead) in *A Fistful of Dollars* (1964). You could spend a long time on Clint. I started by naming five things I loved about him.

1. I love how he holds up four fingers to the coffin maker in *A Fistful of Dollars* and says, "My mistake. Make that four coffins."
2. I love that, as the British critic David Thomson

pointed out, when Clint stood beside Prince Charles at London's National Film Theatre in 1993, it was clear to everyone in the audience who the *real* prince was.

3. I love the fact that when Clint directs a movie, he never says, "Action." He says calmly, quietly, "When you're ready."

4. I love watching Clint fall off his horse in *Unforgiven* (1992).

5. I love the image of Clint, as Dirty Harry, walking down a San Francisco street, gun in one hand, a hot dog in the other.

I mentioned to Jesse a brief junket chat I had once with William Goldman, who did the screenplay for *Butch Cassidy and the Sundance Kid* (1969) and later wrote *Absolute Power* (1997) for Eastwood. Goldman adored him. "Clint is the best," he told me. "A complete professional in a world dominated by ego. On an Eastwood set," he said, "you come to work, you do your job, you go home; usually you go home early because he wants to play golf. And he eats lunch in the cafeteria along with everyone else."

When Clint was offered the script for *A Fistful of Dollars* in 1964, it had already been around for a while. Charles Bronson said no, it was the worst script he'd ever seen. James Coburn didn't want to do it because it was going to be shot in Italy and he'd heard bad things about Italian directors. Clint took it for a fee of fifteen thousand dollars but—and I emphasized this for Jesse—insisted on cutting down the script, thought it would be more interesting if the guy didn't talk.

"Can you guess why he did that?" I said.

"Sure. You imagine all *sorts* of things about a guy who doesn't talk," Jesse said. "The minute he opens his mouth, he shrinks a couple of sizes."

"Exactly.

After a few distracted seconds, he added, "It'd be nice to be like that in real life."

"Huh?"

"Not talk so much. Be more mysterious. Girls like that."

"Some do, some don't," I said. "You're a talker. Women love talkers too."

Three years went by before Eastwood saw the finished film. By then he'd pretty much forgotten about it. He invited some pals to a private screening room and said, "This is probably going to be a real piece of shit, but let's have a look."

A few minutes in, one of his pals said, "Ah, Clint, this is pretty good stuff." *A Fistful of Dollars* revitalized the Western, which had become, at this point, a kind of rest home for aging movie stars.

After the film, I asked Jesse to indulge me, to allow us to revisit the rope scene with James Dean in *Giant*. Dean surrounded by slick businessmen trying to cut him a deal, Rock Hudson laying twelve hundred dollars on the table. "You're in the chips now, boy." Dean just sits there, barely moving. "Who steals the scene?" I asked. "Who steals the whole movie?"

I even made a foray into television—Edward James Olmos as the black-suited police chief in *Miami Vice* (1984–89). I said, "This is a stupid, implausible show, but watch Olmos—it's almost sleight of hand. By not moving, he appears to be in possession of a secret."

"What secret?"

"That's the illusion of stillness. There *is* no secret. Only the implication of a possessor," I said. I was starting to sound like a wine writer.

I clicked off the DVD.

"I wouldn't mind seeing the rest of the show," Jesse said. "Would that be okay?"

So while the contractors banged and sawed and blow-torched the second floor of the condo (getting bigger every day) across the street, Jesse and I watched three consecutive episodes of *Miami Vice*. At one point, our neighbor Eleanor clomped past the window and glanced inside. I wondered what she was thinking, the two of us watching television day after day. I experienced a kind of cretinous desire to run after her, to say, But it's not television; it's *movies*. There was, I noticed in myself, an occasional, unattractive hurry toward explanation these days when it came to Jesse.

———

From where I was standing in the living room, I could see Rebecca Ng turn the corner at the top of the parking lot. White jeans, white jean jacket, chartreuse T-shirt, her night-black hair falling just so. The construction crew at the foot of the church wall signaled to one another and one by one they found a way to look at Rebecca when she got abreast of them. A gray fist of pigeons rose and fluttered to the west.

I was brushing up on New German Cinema. We were doing Werner Herzog's *Aguirre, the Wrath of God* (1972) that day. (Be sure to prepare him for the scene where the conquistador matches his fingers to a bloodstain on a rock.) Sometimes I learned this stuff a half hour before I put the movie on. Jesse was outside. He was hung over. He didn't say it but I had smelled it on him when he came up the stairs. One of his friends, Morgan, had gotten out of jail the night before (thirty days, assault) and dropped by. I'd had to kick him out of the house, gently, at four o'clock in the morning and send Jesse to bed.

It was a fine line *chez nous* and some days I felt like I was beating back chaos and disorder and irresponsibility with a whip and a chair. Indeed, it seemed as if there were a jungle growing all around the house, that it was constantly threatening to poke its branches and vines through the windows, under the door, up through the basement. More than a year had passed since Jesse had left school (he was seventeen now) and there was no sign yet of his charging up the stairs to take the world "by the lapels."

Still we had the film club. The yellow cards on the fridge, a line drawn through each completed film, reassured me that something, at least, was happening. I wasn't delusional. I knew I wasn't giving him a systematic education in cinema. That wasn't the point. We could as easily have gone skin diving or collected stamps. The films simply served as an occasion to spend time together, hundreds of hours, as well as a door-opener for all manner of conversational topics—Rebecca, Zoloft, dental floss, Vietnam, impotence, cigarettes.

Some days, he asked about people I'd interviewed: What was George Harrison like? (A nice guy, although when you hear the Liverpool accent, it's pretty hard not to start jumping around and screaming, "You were in

the Beatles. You must have gotten like a *ton* of chicks!'");
Ziggy Marley (Bob's son, a sullen little prick if there ever
was one); Harvey Keitel (great actor but a brain like an un-
cooked pork roast); Richard Gere (a classic actor-pseudo-
intellectual who hasn't figured out yet that people listen to
him because he's a movie star, not because he's a brainer);
Jodie Foster (like trying to break into Fort Knox); Dennis Hopper (foul-mouthed, funny, a great guy); Vanessa
Redgrave (warm, statuesque, like talking to the Queen);
English director Stephen Frears (another Brit who doesn't
know when to lay off the aftershave; no wonder a woman
can't put her head in these guys' laps); Yoko Ono (a defensive, prickly drag who, when queried about the whys
and wherefores of her latest "project," replied, "Would
you ask Bruce Springsteen that question?"); Robert Alt-
man (chatty, literate, easygoing; no wonder actors worked
for him for a song); American director Oliver Stone (very
masculine guy, smarter than the scripts he writes: "*War
and Peace*? Jesus Christ, what kind of a question is that?
It's ten o'clock in the morning!'").

We talked about the sixties, the Beatles (too often but
he indulged me), drinking badly, drinking well, then some
more about Rebecca ("Do you think she'll dump me?"),
Adolf Hitler, Dachau, Richard Nixon, infidelity, Truman
Capote, the Mojave Desert, Suge Knight, lesbians, cocaine,
heroin chic, the Backstreet Boys (my idea), tattoos, Johnny
Carson, Tupac (his idea), sarcasm, weight lifting, dink size,
French actors, and e. e. cummings. Such a time! I might
have been waiting for a job but I wasn't waiting for life. It
was there, right beside me in the wicker chair. I knew it was

marvelous *while it was happening*—even though I understood, sort of, that the finish line awaited us down the road.

These days, when I return to Maggie's house as a dinner guest, I pause rather tenderly on the porch. I know that Jesse and I will come out here later in the evening with a cup of coffee but it won't be quite the same as it was back then in the film club. Curiously enough, the rest of her house, the kitchen, the bedroom, the living room, and bathroom, bear no trace of me. I feel no resonance, no echo of my time there. Only the porch.

But where was I? Oh yes, Rebecca's visit that fine spring afternoon.

She stepped lightly up the steps; Jesse remained seated. There was an exchange between them; she stood with her hands in her jacket pockets, the expression on her face like that of a stewardess who thinks she has just heard something unpleasant but isn't positive she got it right. A polite but cautious smile. Something unusual going on. In the far distance I could see one of the construction workers, frozen, holding on to the side of a ladder, looking this way.

I heard the door open and they came inside. "Hello, David," Rebecca said. Breezy, in charge. Or at least she wanted to be perceived that way. "How are you feeling today?" she said.

It caught me again by surprise. "How am I feeling? Well, let's see now. Fine, I think. How's school?"

"We're on a little break now so I'm working at the Gap."

"You're going to end up running the world, Rebecca."

"I just like having my own money," she said. (Was that a shot?) Jesse waited behind her.

"Nice to see you again, Rebecca."

"And you too, David," she said. Never "Mr. Gilmour."

Down they went.

I went up to the second floor. Turned on the computer and looked for the third time that day for messages. Maggie was the last person on earth to still use a dial-up Internet phone connection so there was always a wait and buzzing and whining and shrieking before the screen came up.

I read the morning paper online. I looked out the back window and saw our neighbor Eleanor poking about in her back garden with a hoe. Getting ready for a new planting season. Her cherry tree had shot into blossom. After a while I went to the top of the stairs. From the basement I could hear the murmur of conversation. Rebecca's voice, animated; then his, strangely deadpan, too even, as if he were trying to talk from his chest. Talking from an attitude.

Then silence, followed by footsteps on the floor below, two pairs of feet. No words exchanged. The front door opened and closed, carefully, as if someone didn't want to disturb me. By the time I got downstairs I saw Jesse. He was leaning forward, grim-faced. In the distance I spotted a small figure, Rebecca, retreating at the far end of the parking lot. The boys on the construction crew, heads turned in her direction.

I sat down with a creak in the chair. For a moment we just sat there. Then I said, "What's up?"

Jesse turned toward me, holding his hand in a way that obscured his eyes. I wondered if he'd been crying. "We just broke up."

This was what I'd been afraid of. A new guy with a car and

a swanky apartment, a stockbroker, a young lawyer. A more appropriate audience for Rebecca's professional aspirations.

"What did she say?" I said.

"She said she was going to die without me."

For an instant I thought I had misunderstood him. "She said what?"

He repeated it.

"You *dumped* Rebecca?"

He nodded.

"Whatever for?"

"She came over to talk about our relationship one time too many, I guess."

I took a long look at him, his pale complexion, his filmy eyes. After a moment, I said, "I'm sorry to ask this but I have to. Are you hung over today?"

"A bit but that's got nothing to do with it."

"Jesus."

"Really, Dad, it doesn't."

I started in cautiously. "I've learned over the years, Jesse, that it's never a good idea to make a decision about your life when alcohol's involved." He opened his mouth to speak. "Even when it's *indirectly* involved. Like a hangover."

He gazed off into the distance.

"Is there anything you can do to *undo* this?" I said.

"I don't want to." He caught sight of the work crew. It was as if their image reinforced something in him.

I said, "Okay, let me say this and then you can do whatever you want, all right?"

"All right."

"When you leave a woman, things happen that you think

aren't going to matter. But then when they *do* happen, it turns out they matter a great deal."

"Like other guys?"

I said, "I don't want to be brutal about this but there are certain factors you have to take into consideration before you break up with someone. And one of them, the *big* one, it often turns out, is that they're going to be with other people. And that, trust me, can be an unsavory experience."

"What does unsavory mean?"

"Unpleasant. In this case, horrifying."

"I know that Rebecca's going to get another boyfriend, if that's what you mean."

"Do you? Have you really *thought* about it?"

"Yep."

"Can I tell you a story? Do you mind?"

"No, no." He looked distracted. Jesus, I thought. This is just the beginning. "I had a friend in college," I began. "Actually, you know him. He lives on the West Coast. Arthur Cramner."

"I like Arthur."

"Yes, well, a lot of people like Arthur. That was partially the problem. I had a girlfriend once—this was a long time ago; I was maybe a few years older than you are now. Her name was Sally Buckman. And one day I said to Arthur—he was my best friend—'I think I'm going to break up with Sally.' And he said, 'Oh, yeah?' He liked her. Thought she was sexy. She was.

"I said, 'If you want to, you know, *see* Sally afterward, that's fine with me.' I believed it too. I was done with her. So a few weeks later, maybe a month, I broke up with Sally

Buckman and went away for the weekend to a friend's cottage by the lake. Are you still with me?"

"Yep."

I went on. "At that time, Arthur and I played in a rinky-dink band; I played the drums, he sang and played the harmonica; quite the rock stars we fancied ourselves. Slim-hipped irresistibles.

"I got back to town that Sunday night from the cottage, where I'd spent the weekend boiling the roots of marijuana plants and hanging them upside down and not missing Sally one tiny bit. In fact, every so often, I'd feel a gust of relief that she wasn't there.

"I went straight to a band rehearsal. And there was Arthur. Lovely, likable Arthur Cramner, playing the harmonica, kibitzing with the bass guitarist, being a great guy. Being Arthur. All the way through the rehearsal, I kept looking at him, kept wanting to ask him the question 'Did you see Sally while I was away for the weekend?' But I didn't get the chance. I was getting anxious, though. It had moved from being something I was *curious* about to something I was *scared* of.

"So the rehearsal ends, the other guys take off, and I'm sitting in the car with Arthur. Finally I turn to him and say sort of breezily, 'So, did you see Sally this weekend?' And, sounding downright upbeat, he goes, 'Yeah, I did,' as if it's an interesting question to which he has an interesting answer. So I say—and here the words just tumbled out all on their own—'Is there some kind of a *thing* happening there?' And he says, all solemn, 'Yeah, there is.'

"I'll tell you, Jesse. It was as if somebody sped the movie

up ten times. The world just raced by. I could hardly get out a croak. He said, 'Here, have a cigarette.' Which somehow made it worse. I started talking, like super fast, how it was 'all' okay with me but wasn't life strange, didn't things change really fast.

"Then I asked him to drive me over to Sally's. He dropped me off in front of her apartment on Brunswick Street. I still remember the number. I went running up the stairs like there was a fire and knocked, rap, rap, rap; Sally came to the door in her dressing gown, looking, how shall I put it, *cunningly timid*. Like, 'Oh, was there a bomb in that package I sent you?'

"So I ended up in tears, telling her how much I loved her, that I'd 'seen the light.' All that stuff. I just spat it all out in a torrent. I thought I meant every single word too. You get the picture, right?

"So now I'm back with her. I made her throw out the bedsheets and tell me everything that happened. Did you do this, did you do that? Disgusting questions; disgusting answers too." (Here Jesse laughed.) "It took me about a month to remember what a drag she was and then I left again. For good this time. But I made damn sure Arthur was out of town when I did it. I had a feeling she was going to get up to her old tricks and I didn't want him around."

"Did she?"

"She did. She looked up my nutty brother and screwed him. She was bad news, I'm telling you, but that's not the point. The point is sometimes you just don't know how you're going to feel about these things till it's too late. It's not something you want to be rash about."

Eleanor came out on her porch and slipped a wine bottle into the recycling bin. Looked down the street in a pained way, as if she saw something down there she didn't like, rain clouds or vandals, then caught sight of us a few feet away.

"Oh." She jumped. "Hello there, you two. In your office, I see." A furious toothy smile.

Jesse waited till she was gone. "I don't think any of my friends are going to go out with Rebecca."

I said, "The thing is, Jesse, she's going to go with *someone* and, trust me, she's going to make sure you know about it. Have you thought about that?"

In that adult voice of his, a tone lower than usual, he said, "I think it'll be bad for a couple of weeks, then I'll get over it."

I persisted. "Okay then, this is the last thing I'll say and then I'm going to shut up about it. You can *undo* this. You can get on the phone this second and you can get her back here and you can save yourself a lot of discomfort." I let that sink in. "Unless you really don't want her anymore."

Moment's pause. "I don't want her anymore."

"You're sure?"

He looked hesitantly over at the church, at the figures moving around its base. I thought he was having second thoughts. Then he said, "Do you think it was unmasculine for me to have cried?"

"What?"

"When we were breaking up. She was crying too."

"I can imagine."

"But you don't think I was a baby or anything?"

I said, "I think there would have been something wrong

with you, something cold and rather unpleasant, if you *hadn't* cried."

A car drove by.

"Have you ever cried in front of a girl?" he asked.

"The question is, is there a girl I *haven't* cried in front of," I said. When I heard his laughter, when I saw, if only for an instant, the unhappiness vanish from his features (it was like a wind blowing ashes from a beautiful table), it made me feel lighter, as if a mild nausea had passed from my body. If only I could keep him like this, I thought. But I could see, way down the road, images of him waking up at three in the morning and thinking about her, a cement wall toward which he was blindly speeding.

But not for the moment. For the moment we were on the porch, his spirits temporarily lifted from their coffin, to which they would return, like ghosts at sunset, I knew. I was going to show him *Last Tango in Paris* again but it didn't seem like a good idea. The butter scene might lead to all sorts of unhappy imaginings. What then? *Tootsie* (1982), too romantic; *Vanya on 42nd Street* (1994), too Russian; *Ran* (1985), too good to risk his not paying attention. Finally, I got it, a movie that makes you want to take a shotgun and pump a few rounds into the door of your *own* car. A fuck-you movie.

I slipped Michael Mann's *Thief* (1981) into the DVD like it was a nine-millimeter clip. The title sequence rolled (one of the best ever, two guys cracking a safe). Music by Tangerine Dream, a soundtrack like water running through glass pipes. Pastel green, electric pink, neon blue. Watch how the machinery is shot, I said, the love with which blowtorches and drills are lit and photographed; the camera focuses on them with the love of a carpenter viewing his tools.

And James Caan, of course. Never better. Watch for a wonderful moment when he goes into a loan shark's office to get some money and the guy pretends not to know what he's talking about. Watch the pause Caan takes. It's as if he's so furious he has to take a breath to get the sentence out. "I am the last guy on *earth* you want to fuck with," he says.

"Buckle up," I said. "Here we go."

Rebecca returned the next afternoon. She had dressed with great design, black silk shirt, tiny gold buttons, black jeans. She was giving him a last look at dessert before she locked it away. They sat on the porch and talked briefly. I slammed pots and pans in the kitchen at the back of the house, put the radio on loud. I think I even hummed.

The conversation didn't go on for long. When I crept into the living room ("just dusting") for a peek, I saw an odd spectacle. Jesse sat forward in his wicker chair in an attitude of physical discomfort, as if he were waiting for the last seat on a bus, while below him, on the sidewalk, an animated Rebecca (clothed now, it seemed, like a black widow spider) talked to a cluster a teenage boys, all friends of Jesse's who had dropped by. Her manner suggested a graceful and happy ease, not someone who had just lost an appeal, and I realized that there was something dangerous about her. Jesse had sensed it and tired of it. He was, I found myself thinking, a healthier specimen than me. I could never have walked away from a girl that beautiful, from the cocainelike pleasure of having a girlfriend prettier than everyone else's. Petty, dreadful, pitiable, I know. I know.

Soon the porch swarmed with teenage boys. Rebecca was gone. I called Jesse inside and eased the door shut. Quietly I said, "Watch what you say to these guys, all right?"

His pale features looked at me. I could smell the sweat of excitement on him. "You know what she said to me? She said, 'You will never see me again.' "

I waved it away. "That's fine. But promise me you'll watch what you say."

"Sure, sure," he said quickly, but I could tell from the way he said it that he'd already said too much.

CHAPTER

WE HAD A HORROR FESTIVAL. Thinking back, it might have been an insensitive choice—Jesse was probably more fragile than he claimed to be—but I wanted to give him something that would not permit the casual, occasionally saddening introspection that less compelling movies allow. I began with *Rosemary's Baby* (1968), a gothic nightmare about a New Yorker (Mia Farrow) impregnated by the devil. I said to Jesse, "Watch for a famous shot of an old woman"—Ruth Gordon—"talking on the phone. Who's she talking to? But most important, check out the composition of the shot itself. She's half obscured by the door. Why can't we see all of her? Did the director, Roman Polanski, make a mistake or is he trying for an effect?"

I tell Jesse a little about Polanski's painful life; his mother's death in Auschwitz when he was a little boy; his marriage to Sharon Tate, who was pregnant when she was murdered by Charles Manson's followers; his eventual flight from the

United States after a conviction for the statutory rape of a thirteen-year-old girl.

Jesse said, "Do you think somebody should go to jail for having sex with a thirteen-year-old?"

"Yes."

"Don't you think it depends on the thirteen-year-old? I know girls that age who are more experienced than I am."

"Doesn't matter. It's against the law and it should be."

Changing the subject, I mentioned the curious fact that when Polanski drove in the gates of Paramount Pictures on the first day of shooting *Rosemary's Baby*—a major Hollywood film production with real movie stars, Mia Farrow, John Cassavetes, proof that he had "made it"—he felt a strange letdown. I read Jesse this passage from Polanski's autobiography: "I had sixty technicians at my beck and call and bore responsibility for a huge budget—at least by my previous standards—but all I could think of was the sleepless night I'd spent in Krakow, years before, on the eve of making my first short, *The Bicycle*. Nothing would ever match the thrill of that first time."

"What do you make of that story?" I asked.

"That things don't turn out like you think they will."

"But what else?" I prodded.

"That you may be happier *now* than you think you are."

I said, "I used to think my life was going to start when I graduated from university. Then I thought it'd start when I published a novel or got famous or something silly like that." I told him my brother had said this astonishing thing to me once—that he didn't think his life was going to start till he was fifty. "What about you?" I said to Jesse. "When do you think *your* life is going to start?"

"Mine?" Jesse said.

"Yes. Yours."

"I don't believe any of that stuff," he said, rising to his feet in a gust of excitement, the excitement of ideas. "You know what I think? I think your life begins when you're *born*."

He stood in the middle of the living room, almost vibrating. "Do you think that's true? Do you think I'm right?"

"I think you're a very wise man."

And then, in a gesture of uncontrollable pleasure, he clapped his hands together, wham!

"You know what *I* think," I said. "I think you belong in college. That's what they do there. They sit around talking about stuff like this. Except unlike a living room, where there's just your dad, there's a zillion girls."

At that he cocked his head. "Really?"

And like that first day—it seemed ages ago—with *The 400 Blows*, I knew to leave it there.

I showed him next *The Stepfather* (1987), a small-budget film with a silly subplot, but wowie zowie, just wait for the scene where a real estate agent—he's just butchered his own family—takes a buyer for a tour of an empty house; watch his face as he gradually understands it's a therapist he's talking to, not a customer; then *The Texas Chain Saw Massacre* (1974), very poor execution but an idea of such resonating terror that only the subconscious could produce it; then

David Cronenberg's very early *Shivers* (1975). A scientific experiment with parasites goes bad in a bland Toronto high-rise. Sex maniacs stalk the hallways. *Shivers* was the prototype for the exploding stomach years later in *Alien* (1979). I alert Jesse to wait for the final, disturbing shot of larvaelike cars creeping forth from the apartment to spread mayhem. This very low-budget film, curiously erotic, announced the arrival of Cronenberg's unique sensibility: a smart guy with a dirty mind.

We moved on to Hitchcock's *Psycho*. One of the things about a profound experience at the movies is that you remember where you saw it. I saw *Psycho* at the Nortown theater in Toronto when it came out in 1960. I was eleven, and even though I hated scary movies and felt them with an immediacy that alarmed my parents, I went along this time because my best friend was going, a kid with skin as thick as a rhino's.

There are times when you are so frightened that you are paralyzed, when electricity shoots through your body as if you have stuck your finger in a wall socket. That's what happened to me during a couple of the scenes in *Psycho*: not the shower scene itself, because I had my head buried in my arms by then, but rather the moment just *before*, when you can see through the shower curtain that something has come into the bathroom. I remember emerging from the Nortown theater that summer afternoon and thinking that there was something wrong with the sunlight.

On an academic note I mentioned to Jesse that the film was shot—and lit—to look like a cheap exploitation film. I also suggested that *Psycho* was proof that a masterpiece could be flawed. For the moment I didn't say how. (I was thinking of that terrible, talky ending but I wanted him to spot it.)

Then on to a rare film, *Onibaba* (1964). Set in a dreamy world of reeds and marshland in fourteenth-century feudal Japan, this is a black-and-white horror film about a woman and her daughter-in-law who survive by murdering stray soldiers and selling their weapons. But the true subject of the film is sex, its manic lure and the violence it can set off in anyone even close to it. While I was talking I could see Jesse's attention not so much fade as go inside. He was thinking about Rebecca, about what she was up to, with whom, and where.

"What are you thinking about?" I asked.

"About O. J. Simpson," he said. "I'm thinking that if he'd just waited six months, he wouldn't have cared who his wife was with."

I cautioned Jesse to prepare himself for a horrible scene when the old woman tries to tear a devil's mask off her face. (It has shrunk in the rain.) The woman rips and pulls and tugs, blood dripping down her throat, her daughter-in-law smashing, crack, crack, crack, at the mask with a jagged rock. I mention that that very mask later inspired William Friedkin in his physical portrait of the devil in the grand slam of all horror movies, the scariest thing ever made, *The Exorcist* (1973). That was next on the list and it really finished us off.

The first time I saw *The Exorcist*, I was twenty-four and it scared me so badly I fled the theater a half hour in. A few days later I crept back and tried again. I got to the halfway mark, but when the little girl slowly rotated her head, accompanied by the sounds of cracking sinews, I felt as if my blood had turned cold, and I beat it again. It was only the third time that I went the distance, peeking through my fingers and plugging my ears with my thumbs. Why did I keep going back? Because I had a feeling this was a "great" movie—not intellectually because I'm not sure even its director cared about the ideas in it, but because it was a one-of-a-kind artistic achievement. The work of a prodigiously gifted director at the height of his artistic maturity.

I also pointed out that Friedkin, who had just come from directing *The French Connection*, was, by many accounts, a bully and a borderline psycho. The crew referred to him as "Wacky Willie." A director from the old school, he screamed at people, foamed at the mouth, fired staff in the morning and rehired them in the afternoon. He shot off guns on the set to scare the actors and played insane tapes—South American tree frogs or the soundtrack from *Psycho*—at nerve-jarring volume. It kept everyone nicely on edge.

Single-handedly he drove the budget of *The Exorcist* — which was supposed to be four million dollars—straight through the ceiling to twelve million. One day, while shooting in New York, he was reportedly doing a close-up of bacon cooking on a griddle and didn't like how the bacon was curling; he brought the shoot to a close while they hunted around New York for some preservative-free bacon that would remain flat. Friedkin worked so slowly that a crew member who got sick came back to the set after three days to find they were still on the same bacon shot.

The producers wanted Marlon Brando to play the role of Father Merrin, the senior exorcist, but Friedkin was concerned, paranoid, some might say, that that might make it "a Brando film" rather than his. (Ungenerous souls had said the same thing to Francis Coppola about *The Godfather*, which had just come out.)

There was a story going around for years that during one scene where he was using a nonactor to play a priest (the man was a priest in real life), Friedkin wasn't getting the performance he wanted. So he asked the priest, "Do you trust me?" The man of God said yes, whereupon Willie drew back and smacked him across the face. Friedkin got the "take" he wanted. You can see it when Father Damien is getting the last rites at the foot of the stairs. The priest's hands are still shaking.

Talent, as I had said earlier to Jesse, does indeed take hold in strange and sometimes undeserving nooks. Friedkin might have been a cretin, I pointed out, but you couldn't knock his visual sense. Every time that camera starts up the stairs to the child's room, you know it's going to be something new and horrible and worse than the time before.

Jesse slept on the couch that night, two lamps on. Next morning, both of us mildly embarrassed about the horrors of the evening before, we agreed to suspend the festival for a while. Great comedies, bad girls, Woody Allen, nouvelle vague, anything. Just no more horror. There are moments in *The Exorcist*, the little girl sitting on the bed, very still, speaking calmly in a man's voice, when it feels as if you are teetering on the brink of a place you should *never* visit.

CHAPTER

IN READING OVER WHAT I'VE WRITTEN, I realize that I may have given the impression that I had little else going on in my life except watching movies and kibitzing at the side of my son's life. That wasn't the case. I was getting a little work by now, book reviews, a documentary that needed polish, even a few days of substitute teaching (dismaying by implication, of course, but not the vanity-smashing experience I'd feared).

I sold my loft in the candy factory and with the windfall that came with it, my wife and I bought a Victorian house on the edge of Chinatown. Maggie finally returned home. Such happiness; it had been more than a year. She still, however, felt Jesse needed to "live with a man." So did I. So, mercifully, did my wife. At a family party over Christmas, a diminutive, sparrow-voiced aunt, the retired principal of a high school, had told me, "Don't be fooled. Teenage boys need as much attention as newborns. Except they need it from their *fathers*."

Jesse followed me and Tina across town with three industrial-strength garbage bags of clothing and dozens of caseless CDs. He moved into the blue bedroom on the third floor, from which you could see all the way to the lake. It was the best room in the house, the quietest, the best ventilated. I bought him a print of John Waterhouse's naked maidens swimming in a pond and hung it on his wall between posters of Eminem (a homely-looking fellow when all is said and done), Al Pacino with a cigar (*Scarface*), and some thug wearing nylons on his head and pointing a nine-millimeter pistol in your face, the caption reading: SAY HELLO TO DA BAD GUYZ.

In fact, as I write this, I am only a few yards down the hall from Jesse's blue bedroom, empty now, one of his discarded shirts still hanging on the back of the door. The room is tidier these days, a DVD of *Chungking Express* (1994) ranged away in his night table alongside *Middlemarch* (still unread), Elmore Leonard's *Glitz* (at least he didn't sell it), Tolstoy's *The Cossacks* (my idea), and Anthony Bourdain's *The Nasty Bits*, which he left here the last time he and his girlfriend spent the night. I find the presence of these things comforting, as if he is still here, in spirit anyway; that he will, indeed, be back someday.

Still, and I don't want to get maudlin here, some nights I walk by his bedroom on the way to my study and I take a peek inside. The moonlight falls over his bed, the room is very still, and I can't quite believe he's gone. There were other things we were going to do to that room, other prints, another clothes peg for the wall. But time ran out.

Fall in Chinatown; the leaves turning red in the giant for-
ests north of the city. Gloves appeared on the hands of the
women who rode their bicycles past our house. Jesse got a
part-time job working the phones for a pair of telemarketing
slimeballs who raised money for a "firemen's magazine."

Early one evening, I stopped by the "office," a grungy
little joint with six or seven compartments in which sat a
dead-end white kid, a Pakistani, an overweight woman with
a tub of Coke in front of her, all working the phones. Jesus,
I thought. This is the company I've dropped him into. This
is the future.

And there he was, right at the back, phone to his ear, his
voice hoarse from hustling seniors and shut-ins and gull-
ibles at dinnertime. He was good at phone sales, you could
tell. He got people on the phone and held them there and
charmed them and made them laugh and kidded them until
they coughed it up.

The bosses were there too, a runt in a yellow windbreaker
and his smoothie partner, a good-looking con named Dale.
I introduced myself. Jesse was their top boy, they said. Number one on the "floor." Behind us, I heard snatches of barely
comprehensible English, an Eastern European voice with an
accent so thick it sounded like a sitcom; Bengali drifted over
from a different booth; then a woman's nasal voice, punctu-
ated by the sound of someone sucking ice cubes through a
straw. It sounded like a shovel on cement.

Jesse came over, that jaunty walk he had when he was
happy, looking left and right. He said, "Let's go outside

for a chat," which meant he didn't want me talking too long to his bosses, making inquiries about the "firemen's magazine." As in, Is there a copy I might have a look at? (There wasn't.)

I took him to dinner at Le Paradis that same night. (If I had an addiction, it wasn't booze or cocaine or girlie mags; it was eating in restaurants even when I was broke.)

"Have you ever actually *seen* this firemen's magazine?" I asked. He chewed his flatiron steak for a moment, his mouth open. Maybe it was the poorly digested nap I'd taken that afternoon but just the fact of him eating with his mouth open after I'd told him four thousand times not to plunged me into an irritable despair.

"Jesse," I said, "please."

"What?" he said.

I made a rather coarse gesture with my lips.

Normally he would have laughed (even if it wasn't amusing) and said sorry and gone on with things, but tonight there was a hesitation. I saw his face go slightly white. He looked down at his plate as if he were making a decision, a tough one, to overcome a bodily sensation. Then he said simply, "Okay." But you could feel the heat still in the air. It was as if I had opened a furnace door and then shut it.

"If you don't want me to correct your table manners . . ." I began.

"It's fine," he said, waving it away. Not looking at me. I thought, Oh, God, I've mocked him. I've offended his pride by making that stupid face. For a moment the two of us sat there, him chewing, staring at his plate, me looking at him with crumbling determination. "Jesse," I said gently.

"Huh?" He looked up, but not the way you look at your father, more the way Al Pacino looks at an asshole in *Carlito's Way*. We had passed a stage somewhere. He was sick of being scared of me and wanted me to know it. In fact, the balance was shifting even more dramatically. I was becoming intimidated by *his* displeasure.

I said, "Do you want to go outside for a cigarette, cool down?"

"I'm fine."

I said, "That was coarse what I just did. I'm sorry."

"That's all right."

"I want you to forgive me for it—okay?"

He didn't answer. He was thinking about something else.

"Okay?" I repeated softly.

"Okay, sure. Done."

"What?" I asked, even more softly. He was dangling his napkin from his hand, just brushing it back and forth, back and forth over a spot on the table. Was he remembering that scene with James Dean twirling the rope? Saying no to whatever was being asked of him.

"Sometimes I think you have too big an effect on me," he said.

"How do you mean?"

"I don't think other kids get so"—he looked for the word—"paralyzed by having a fight with their dads. Some of them tell them to fuck off."

"I don't ever want us to be like that," I said, nearly breathless.

"No, me neither. But shouldn't I be a little less *affected* by you?"

"Are you?"

"It's why I don't get in trouble. I'm terrified of you being mad at me."

This was not the conversation I had planned when I had invited him out to a dinner I could not afford.

"Terrified of what? I've never hit you. I've never—" I stopped.

"I'm like a little kid." His eyes misted up with frustration. "I shouldn't be so nervous around you."

I put down my fork. I could feel the color flee my face. "You have more power over me than you think."

"Do I?"

"Yes."

"Like when?"

"Like right now."

"Do you think you have *too* much power over me?" he said.

I was having trouble catching my breath. I said, "I think you want me to think well of you."

"You don't think I'm just a little baby who's scared of you?"

"Jesse, you're six foot four. You could beat the—forgive my language—shit out of me whenever you wanted to."

"Do you think I could?"

"I know you could."

Something in his whole body relaxed. He said, "I want that cigarette now," and went outside. I could see him moving back and forth on the other side of the French doors, and after a while he came back in and said something to the bartender, who laughed, and then came up through the room, a dark-haired college girl watching him carefully. I could see he was happy, looking left and right, a bounce back in his step, settling back down at the table, picking up his napkin, wiping his mouth. I've given him what he needs for now, I thought, but he'll need more soon.

I said, "Can we talk about the firemen's magazine?"

"Sure," he said, pouring himself a fresh glass of wine. (Usually I poured.) "I love this restaurant," he said. "If I were rich, I think I'd have dinner here every night."

Things were definitely changing between us. I knew down the road, not that far, we were going to have a shootout and I was going to lose. Just like all those other fathers in history. It's how I picked our next movie.

Do you remember those words "I know what you're thinkin'—did he fire six shots or only five? Well, to tell you the truth, in all this excitement I kinda lost track myself. But being this is a forty-four Magnum, the most powerful handgun in the world, and would blow your head clean off, you gotta ask yourself one question: 'Do I feel lucky?' Well, do you, punk?"

When the good Lord calls Clint Eastwood home, that speech will turn up on every six o'clock news show around the world, Dirty Harry looking down the barrel of his gun at an out-of-luck bank robber and giving him the business. That movie—if not that speech—shot Clint Eastwood into the front ranks of American leading men, up there with John Wayne and Marlon Brando. A year later, in 1973, a screenwriter phoned Clint Eastwood, said he'd been reading about the death squads in Brazil, rogue cops killing criminals without bothering to take them to court. How about Dirty Harry discovering the presence of death squads in the LAPD? They'd call it *Magnum Force*.

The movie was on; when it opened during the holiday season the following year, it sold even more tickets than *Dirty Harry*; in fact, it made more money for Warner Bros. in its first weeks than any previous film in its history.

Magnum Force is by far the best of the *Dirty Harry* sequels and cemented the love affair between movie audiences and the gun that could "blow the engine block out of a car at a hundred yards."

"But," I said to Jesse, "that's not why I'm showing it to you."

"No?" he said.

I stopped the film in midframe right near the beginning, where Inspector "Dirty" Harry Callahan steps off the sidewalk of a sunny street in San Francisco and approaches a murder victim's car, the body inside, major head wound. Behind Eastwood, on the sidewalk, is a long-haired, bearded man.

I said, "Do you recognize him?"

"No."

"That's my brother," I said.

It was indeed my estranged brother, who happened to be passing through San Francisco when the film was being shot. He had driven west in a wild flurry, four days, to join a religious cult, I've forgotten which one. But when he knocked at their door he was refused entry. So he bought a ticket for a live taping of *The Merv Griffin Show* and did that instead. Then just as fast as he'd arrived, he took off back to Toronto. But sometime that first day, he wandered into a film shoot.

"That's your uncle," I said.

We both scrutinized the screen; behind the shaggy hair and beard was a handsome young man, twenty-five years old, who looked like Kris Kristofferson.

"Have I ever met him?" Jesse asked.

"Once, when you were little, he turned up at the door. Wanting something. I remember sending you back inside."

"Why?"

I looked again at the screen. "Because," I said, "my brother had a genius for stirring up trouble between people. I didn't want him poisoning your ear when you were fourteen and ready to hear some bad things about me. So I kept him from you."

Then we turned the movie back on; the freeze frame melted, the movie moved forward, and my brother disappeared from the screen.

"But that's not the only reason," I said. "The real reason is that when I was smaller than him, he scared the hell out of me. And you end up hating people who scare you. Do you understand what I'm saying to you?"

"Yeah."

"I don't want that to happen with us," I said. "Please."

Just that "please" gave him something a hundred apologies or explanations couldn't.

There was no firemen's magazine; it was a scam. A few weeks later, when Jesse went in to "work," the place was locked up, Dale and the runt gone. They beat him for a few hundred dollars but he didn't seem to care. The job had served its purpose, the first steps in a break from his dependence on his parents. (He understood intuitively, I think, that financial dependence cements emotional dependence.)

There were other, worse jobs around, and before long he found one. Another telemarketing gig, this one selling credit cards to poor families in the Deep South, Georgia, Tennessee, Alabama, Mississippi. I wasn't invited around to meet the boss. Some nights when he returned home, his voice ravaged from talking and smoking, I'd quiz him. I'd say, "Explain to me why MasterCard would entrust a bunch of young guys in baseball hats to sell credit cards. I don't get it."

"Neither do I, Dad," he said, "but it works."

Meanwhile there was not a hint of Rebecca—not a sighting in a club, on the street, no phone calls, nothing. It was as if she had developed a kind of radar that warned her when Jesse was nearby and she simply vanished. When she said, "You will never see me again," she had been true to her word.

I awoke one night for no particular reason. My wife was asleep beside me with an expression on her face as if she were trying to solve a math problem in her head. Wide awake and mildly anxious, I looked out the window. There was a circle of mist around the moon. I put on my dressing gown and went down the stairs. An open DVD box lay on the chesterfield. Jesse must have come in late and watched a movie after we had gone to bed. I went over to the machine to see what it was but as I drew closer I experienced a kind of foreboding, as if I were crossing a line into a dangerous zone, that I was going to find something I wouldn't like. A gruesomely pornographic movie maybe, something to shore up my confidence in the effectiveness of my childrearing.

But perversity, annoyance, a sense of supervisory impatience, I don't know what, overcame my caution, and I popped open the tray. And what came out? Not what I expected. It was the small Hong Kong film, *Chungking Express*, which I'd shown Jesse months before. Images of a celery-stick Asian girl dancing alone around a stranger's apartment. What was the song? Oh yes, "California Dreamin'," the Mamas and the Papas hit, sounding fresh and *big* in a way it never had in the sixties.

I felt a peculiar alertness, a tugging at my sleeve, as if I were staring at something but couldn't recognize what it was. Like the priceless stamps in Stanley Donen's *Charade* (1963). What *was* it?

Somewhere in the house, I could hear something very faint, a clicking. I went up the stairs; it got louder; then up to the third floor. I was going to knock on his door—you don't go into a young man's bedroom in the middle of the night unannounced—when I saw him through a crack in the door.

"Jesse?" I whispered.

No answer. The room was washed in a green light, Jesse at the computer, his back to me. The sound of insects coming from the headphones on his ears. He was writing somebody. A private moment, click-click, click, click-click, but such a lonely one, four o'clock in the morning, writing to some other kid thousands of miles away; talking about what? Rap, sex, suicide? And again I saw him standing at the bottom of a glistening well, mortar and brick all the way around, no way to climb up (too slippery), no way to break through (too hard), just an eternity of waiting for something to appear overhead, a cloud, a face, a rope dangled down.

And I understood suddenly why the movie had caught my attention, why that particular movie, *Chungking Express*. Because the beautiful girl in it reminded him of Rebecca; and watching the movie was a little bit like being with her.

I went back upstairs and went to sleep. Terrible dreams. A boy in a damp well, waiting.

He didn't get up until my third call the next afternoon. I went upstairs and gave his shoulder a gentle shake. He was sleeping too deeply. It took him twenty minutes to make it downstairs. Leaves falling from the trees in the late-afternoon sunlight. Almost a marine look, as if, with the bright golds and greens, we were underwater. A pair of running shoes (a prank) hung from a power line overhead. Down the street were more. A boy in a red T-shirt cycled by, swooping in and out of the little piles of leaves. Jesse seemed listless.

I was going to say but didn't, "I think you should start going to the gym."

He pulled out a cigarette.

"Please, not before breakfast."

He sat forward, rocking his head slightly back and forth. "Do you think I should call Rebecca?" he said.

"Is she still on your mind?" (Stupid question.)

"Every second of every day. I think I made a big mistake."

After a moment I said, "I think Rebecca was big trouble and you got out before the house burned down."

I could see he wanted a cigarette, that he wasn't going to concentrate till he had one. I said, "Light up if you want to. You know it makes me ill."

Calmer once the smoke filled his lungs (his complexion even grayer, it seemed), he said, "Is this going to go on forever?"

"What?"

"Missing Rebecca."

I thought of Paula Moors, an old heartbreak of my own; I lost twenty pounds in two weeks over her. "It's going to go on until you find someone you like as much as her," I said.

"Not just another girlfriend?"

"No."

"What if she's just a nice person? That's what my mom says."

That remark—with its attendant implications that a "nice" girl would make Jesse forget his sexual longing for Rebecca—captured a side of Maggie that was both endearing and maddening. Here was a woman who had taught high school in a small Saskatchewan farming community, who, at the age of twenty-five, decided she wanted to be an actress, quit her job, bid her family a tearful, train-station good-bye, and came to Toronto—two thousand miles away—to do it.

When I met her she had green hair and was appearing in a punk musical. But somehow, when she talked to our son about his life, especially his "future," she forgot all that and became instead a spouter of breathtakingly simple-minded counsel. ("Maybe you should go to math camp this summer.") Her worry, her concern for his welfare, Nova-cained her intelligence, which was normally intuitive and considerable.

What she did best for Jesse she did by example, imparting a democratic kindness, a giving-people-the-benefit-of-the-doubt that his father, occasionally too hasty with a condemning turn of phrase, did not.

In a word, she sweetened his soul.

"Your mother means well," I said, "but she's wrong there."

"You figure I'm addicted to Rebecca?" he said.

"Not literally."

"What if I never find anyone I'm that attracted to?"

I thought again of Paula Moors and her fat-burning exit; she was a brunette with vaguely crooked teeth, the kind of flaw that can give a woman an eerie sex appeal. God how I missed her. Yearned for her. Suffered grotesque imaginings that made me change my T-shirt in the middle of the night.

I said, "You remember Paula? You were ten when she left."

"She used to read to me."

"I thought I'd be haunted by her for the rest of my life, no matter who I was with. That there would always be a *Yes, but she's not Paula*."

"And?"

I chose my words carefully, not wanting things to get locker-roomy. "It wasn't the first woman or the second or the third woman. But when it happened, when the chemistry was right and things worked out, I never gave Paula another thought."

"You were kind of a mess for a while there."

"You remember that?" I said.

"Yep."

"What do you remember?"

"I remember you falling asleep on the couch after dinner."

I said, "I was taking sleeping pills. Big mistake." Pause. "You had to put yourself to bed a few times, didn't you?"

I thought of that awful spring, the sunlight too bright, me walking through the park like a skeleton, Jesse darting timid glances up at me. He said once, taking my hand, "You're starting to feel better, aren't you, Dad?" This little ten-year-old boy looking after his father. Jesus.

"I'm like that guy in *Last Tango in Paris*," Jesse said. "Wondering if his wife did the same things with the guy in the dressing gown downstairs that she did with him." I could feel him looking at me uncertainly, unsure whether to go on. "Do you think that's true?" he asked.

I knew what he was thinking about. "I don't think there's any point in thinking about that stuff," I said.

But he needed more. His eyes searched my face as if he were looking for a very small dot. I remembered nights lying in bed forcing myself to visualize the most pornographic images imaginable, Paula doing this, Paula doing that. I did it to blunt my nerve endings, to hurry to the finish line, to that point where I wouldn't give a shit what she did with her fingers or what she put in her mouth. Etc., etc.

"Getting over a woman has its own timetable, Jesse. It's like growing your fingernails. You can do anything you want, pills, other girls, go to the gym, don't go to the gym, drink, don't drink, it doesn't seem to matter. You don't get to the other side *one second faster.*"

He looked across the street; our Chinese neighbors were working in the garden, calling out to each other. "I should have waited until I had another girlfriend," he said.

"She might have canned you first. Think about that."

He stared ahead for a moment, his long elbows on his knees, picturing God knows what. "What do you think about me phoning her?"

I opened my mouth to reply. I remembered waking up early one gray February morning after Paula was gone, wet snow sliding down the window, and thinking I'd go mad from the endlessness of that day ahead of me. *This is delicate flesh you are dealing with. Tread softly.*

"You know what she'll do, don't you?" I said.

"What?"

"Punish you. She'll reel you in and in and in and just when you think you're home free, she'll bring down the curtain."

"You figure?"

"She's not stupid, Jesse. She'll know exactly what it is you want. And she won't give it to you."

"I just want to hear her voice."

"I doubt that," I said, but then I looked over at his unhappy features, at the flatness that seemed to have overtaken his whole body. Softly, I said, "I think you'll be sorry if you start up with her again. You're almost at the finish line."

"What finish line?"

"Getting over her."

"No, I'm not. I'm not even *nearly* there."

"You're farther along than you think."

"How do you know that? I don't mean to be rude, Dad, but how do you know that?"

"Because I've done it about three million times, that's how I know," I said sharply.

"I'm never going to get over her," he said, abandoning himself to despair. I could feel prickles of irritation, almost like sweat, on my skin—not because he was questioning me, but because he was unhappy and I couldn't do anything, nothing, to relieve him of it. It made me angry at him, like wanting to strike a child who falls down and hurts himself. He shot a glance at me, one of those I remembered from years ago, a worried look that said, Uh-oh, he's getting mad at me.

I said, "It's like the guy who gives up cigarettes. A month goes by, he gets drunk, he figures, What the hell? Halfway through the second cigarette he remembers why he gave it up. But now he's smoking again. So he has about ten thousand more cigarettes before he arrives back at precisely the same place he was at before he lit up."

Jesse put his hand awkwardly, tenderly, on my shoulder and said, "I can't give up cigarettes either, Dad."

CHAPTER 10

No MORE THAN A FEW DAYS LATER, I had dinner with Maggie. I'd ridden my bicycle over to her house in Greektown earlier in the evening, but after dinner, after the wine, I had no desire to risk a wobbly drive back across the bridge into town. So I clambered aboard the subway with the bike in tow.

It wasn't a long trip home, ten or fifteen minutes, but I'd done it so many times it seemed intolerably sluggish and I was sorry not to have brought a book to read. I was gazing at my reflection in the window, at the passengers coming and going, the tunnels whizzing by, when who should I see but Paula Moors? She was sitting opposite me, five or six rows down the subway car. I don't know how long she'd been there, or where she got on. I stared at her profile for a moment, the sharp nose, the pointed jaw. (I'd heard she got her teeth straightened.) Her hair was longer now, but she looked unchanged, very much as she had delivering those terrible words: "I'm leaning toward not being in love with you." What a sentence! What a choice of words!

For six months, maybe a year, I've forgotten, I had felt her absence with the acuity of a toothache. We had committed such middle-of-the night intimacies, she and I, private things said, private things done, and now the two of us sat unspeaking on the same subway train. Which would have struck me as tragic when I was younger but now seemed, I don't know, rather ruefully true to life. Not fantastic or sad or obscene or hilarious, just sort of business-as-usual, the mystery of someone coming and going in your life not so mysterious after all. (They have to go somewhere.)

And how, I wondered (an East Indian woman getting off at the Broadview station), how could I make Jesse understand this, how could I rush him through the next months, even year, to that delicious end point where you wake up one day and instead of feeling her loss (that toothache), you find yourself, yawning, putting your hands behind your head, and thinking, I must get a copy made of my house key today. I'm playing a rather dangerous game here, having only one key. Gorgeously banal, liberating thoughts (Did I lock the downstairs window?), the heat having passed from the burn, the memory of its pain so remote that you can't quite put your finger on why it went on so long or what the fuss was about, or who did what with her body (But look—the neighbors are planting a new birch tree).

As if the chain on an anchor has snapped (you can't quite remember where you were or what you were doing), you notice suddenly that your thoughts are your own possession again; your bed no longer empty but simply yours, yours in which to read the newspaper or sleep or . . . dear me, what *was* it I was supposed to do today? Ah, the front-door key! Yes.

How to get Jesse there?

And looking around the subway car (a young woman eating a bag of potato chips getting on), I noticed that Paula had gone. Had gotten off at an earlier stop. I had, I realized with mild surprise, forgotten that she was there, the two of us whistling through darkened tunnels, the two of us so engaged *elsewhere* that we—I was sure this applied to her as well—had gotten used to and then indifferent to the presence of the other, all in a matter of five minutes. How—*what*? How *odd*. I suppose that's the word. But even that thought was immediately replaced. As I walked my bike along the platform, the train moving away from me, I noticed that the girl with the potato chips had braces on her teeth. She ate with her mouth open.

Jesse got up before noon one day, an event that I celebrated by showing him *Dr. No* (1962). It was the first James Bond film. I tried to explain to him the excitement those Bond movies caused when they first appeared. They seemed so urbanely scented, so naughty. There's a certain effect films have on you when you're very young, I explained; they give you an imaginative experience in a way that is hard to recapture when you're older. You "buy it" in a way that you can't really later.

When I go to a movie now, I seem to be aware of so many more things: the man a few rows over talking to his wife, someone finishing his popcorn and throwing the bag into the aisle; I'm aware of editing and bad dialogue and second-rate actors. Sometimes I watch a scene with a lot of extras and I wonder, Are they real actors, are they enjoying being extras or are they unhappy not to be in the spotlight? There's a young girl, for example, in the communications center at the beginning of *Dr. No*. She has one or two lines but you never see her on the screen again. I wondered out loud to Jesse what happened to all those people in those crowd shots, those party shots: How did their lives turn out? Did they give up acting and go into other professions?

All these things interfere with the experience of a movie; in the old days you could have fired off a pistol beside my head and it wouldn't have interrupted my concentration, my participation in the movie that was unfolding on the screen in front of me. I return to old movies not just to watch them again but in the hope that I'll feel the way I did when I first saw them. (Not just about movies, but about everything.)

———————————

Jesse looked shaky when he came outside onto the porch. It was November again, a few days till his eighteenth birthday. How was that possible? It seemed like his birthday came every four months now, as if time were indeed giving me the bum's rush to the grave.

I asked him about his evening; yes, all fine, nothing special, though. Dropped over to see a friend. Uh-huh. Which friend?

Pause. "Dean."

"I don't know Dean, do I?"

"Just a fellow."

Fellow? (You hear language that out of character, you want to call the police.) He could tell I was looking at him.

"What did you do then?"

"Not much; watched some television; it was all a bit boring." There was in his answers the feeling of somebody trying to stay off the radar screen, of somebody not wanting the conversation to catch like a shirt on a nail. A woman with a prematurely aged face passed by on the sidewalk.

"She should dye her hair," Jesse said.

"You seem a bit fragile today," I said. "What were you drinking last night?"

"Just beer."

"No hard liquor?"

"A bit, yes."

"What kind?"

"Tequila."

I said, "Tequila leaves a very bad hangover."

"It sure does."

Another silence. It was a strangely motionless day. The sky white as a board.

I said, "Were there any drugs involved during this tequila evening?"

"No," he said offhandedly. Then: "Yes, there were."

"What kind of drugs, Jesse?"

"I don't want to lie to you, okay?"

"Okay."

Pause. The windup. Then the pitch. "Cocaine."

The woman with the old face came back this way carrying a little plastic bag of groceries.

"I feel so terrible," he said. For an instant I thought he was going to burst into tears.

"Cocaine can leave you feeling very sordid," I said softly and rested my hand on his thin shoulder.

He sat up quickly as if responding to his name being called out at roll call. "That's it, that's exactly it. I feel so sordid."

"This was where, at Dean's?"

"His name's not Dean." Pause. "It's Choo-choo."

What the hell kind of a name is that? "What does this Choo-choo do for a living?" I said.

"He's a white rapper."

"Yeah?"

"Yeah. Absolutely."

"He's a working musician?"

"Not exactly."

"So he's a coke dealer?"

Another pause. Another rallying of troops that had long since decamped. "I went back to his house last night. He just kept bringing it out."

"And you kept doing it?"

He nodded, gazing numbly down the street.

"Have you been to Choo-choo's house before?"

"I don't really want to talk about this now," he said.

"I don't give a shit if you want to talk about it now or not. Have you been to Choo-choo's house before?"

"No. Honest."

"Ever done coke before?"

"Not like this."

"Not like *this*?"

"No."

I said, after a moment, "Didn't we have a talk about this stuff?"

"About coke?"

I said, "You know what I'm talking about."

"Yes, we did."

"That if I caught you doing drugs, the deal's off. Rent, pocket money, all of it, over. You remember that?"

"Yep."

"Did you think I was kidding?"

"No, but one thing, Dad. You didn't *catch* me. I told you."

I didn't have an immediate answer for that one. After a while I said, "Did you phone anybody?"

He looked surprised. "How did you know?"

"That's what people do when they're on coke. They get on the phone. And they're always sorry. Who'd you call? Did you call Rebecca?"

"No."

"Jesse?"

"I tried to. She wasn't in." He slumped forward in his chair. "How long is this going to go on?"

"How much did you do?"

"All night. He just kept bringing it out."

I went into the house and got a sleeping pill from my sock drawer and brought it back outside with a glass of water. I said, "This is a one-shot number, okay? You do this again, you're going to have to suffer through it." I gave him the pill, told him to swallow.

"What is it?" he said.

"Doesn't matter." I waited till he swallowed and I had his attention. I said, "We're not going to talk about this right now, okay? You understand what I'm saying?"

"Yep."

I kept him company until he got drowsy from the sleeping pill. It made him a little loose-tongued.

"Do you remember that speech in the *Under the Volcano* documentary?" he asked. "Where the consul is going on about his hangover, about hearing people coming and going outside the window, repeating his name scornfully?"

I said I did, yes.

He said, "That happened to me this morning. Just when I was waking up. Do you think I'm going to end up like that guy?"

"No."

Then he went upstairs. I tucked him in. I said, "You're going to be a bit depressed when you wake up."

"Are you mad at me?"

"Yep. I am."

I hung around the house that afternoon. He came downstairs sometime after dark. He was famished. We ordered from Chicken Chalet. When it was done, wiping the grease from his lips, from his fingers, he lay back on the couch. "I said some pretty stupid things last night," he said. Then he went on, as if he needed to torture himself. "I thought I was some kind of a rock star there for a while." He groaned. "You ever do something like that?"

I didn't answer him. He wanted, I could tell, to lure me into some kind of complicity. But I wasn't playing.

He said, "It was just getting light when I left Choochoo's. And there were all these pizza boxes lying all over the place, this really shitty apartment, excuse my language, a real dump. I saw myself in the mirror. You know what I was wearing? Some kind of bandanna around my head."

He pondered it all a moment longer. "Don't tell my mother, all right?"

"I'm not going to keep secrets from your mother, Jesse. You tell me something, I'm going to tell her."

He took it calmly. Slightly nodding his head. No surprise, no resistance. I don't know what he was thinking; remembering something that had gotten said the night before, some grotesque posturing, some unattractive vanity one is always prudent to keep private. But I wanted to sweeten his soul, to banish the image of pizza boxes and crappy apartments and all the ugly things he must have thought about himself coming home on the subway at the crack of dawn, everybody else around him fresh and awake to a new day. I wanted to turn him inside out and hose down his insides with warm water.

But how sunny *is* he inside there? I wondered. This boy with the jaunty walk. Do I have any idea what the rooms in that mansion *really* look like? I fancy I do but sometimes, listening to him on the phone downstairs, I hear a foreignness in his voice, a harshness, even sometimes a coarseness, and I ask myself, Is that him? Or is that a posture? Or is the face he turns to *me* a posture? Who was that kid on coke in the crappy apartment, coming on like a bullying rock star? Do I ever see *that* guy?

I said, "I got something I want to show you," and went over to the DVD player.

In a very fragile voice, a voice that wants trouble from no one, a voice that expects perfect strangers to slap you in the face, he said, "I don't think I can watch a movie right now, Dad."

"I know you can't. So I'm just going to play you *one* scene. It's from an Italian movie. My mother's favorite. She used to play the soundtrack over and over at our summer cottage. I'd come up from the dock and hear this music coming from our house and I'd know my mother'd be sitting on the screened-in deck, drinking a gin and tonic and listening to this record. I always think about her when I hear this music. It always makes me happy, I don't know why. It must have been a good summer.

"Anyway, I'm going to show you the very last scene in the movie. I think you'll figure out why pretty fast. This guy—he's played by Marcello Mastroianni—has been drinking and whoring and generally pissing his life away night after night, and he ends up on a beach at sunrise with a bunch of partygoers. You reminded me of it with that business about the pizza boxes lying all over Choo-choo's apartment.

"So there he is on the beach, hungover, still in his party clothes, and he hears a young girl calling him. He looks over, sees her, but he can't hear what she's saying. She's so beautiful, so pure, it's like she's the embodiment of the sea and the bright morning, maybe even the embodiment of his own childhood. I want you to watch this scene and remember this. This guy, this party guy, his life has already peaked, he's on the way downhill; he knows it, the girl on the beach knows it. But *you*, your life, it's just starting, it's all ahead of you. It's yours to throw away."

I put on Federico Fellini's *La Dolce Vita* (1960) and jumped to the last scene, Mastroianni walking ankle deep in the sand, the girl fifty yards away calling to him across a little patch of water. He shrugs, makes a gesture with his hands: I don't understand, it says. He starts to walk away; his friends are waiting. He waves good-bye to the girl, this funny little wave, his fingers sort of bent. It's as if his hand is somehow curdled. *He's* curdled. The girl watches him walk away; she's still smiling, first with kindness, with understanding, but then with firmness. She seems to be saying, Okay, if that's the way you want it. But then very slowly she turns her glance straight into the camera. And you, the glance says to the audience, what about your life?

"The one thing I want to say to you about cocaine," I said, "is that it always ends up this way."

We watched *It's a Wonderful Life* (1946) the next morning. I knew he'd hate it at first, the overenergized acting, its falseness, James Stewart's self-conscious adorableness. Jesse wouldn't buy any of that. Particularly in that state, seeing the world like some kind of—what did we call it at his age—oh yes, seeing the world like some kind of "cosmic bargain basement."

But when the movie turns dark, and James Stewart

darkens with it (how disturbing he is, like somebody throwing a drink in somebody's face at your parents' party), I knew Jesse would be hooked, in spite of himself. He'd have to know how it ends, he'd have to know for his own sake, because by that time the story on the screen would have become *his* story. And can anyone, even a depressed teenager with a cocaine and tequila hangover, resist the film's final moments?

He got a job washing dishes in a restaurant up on St. Clair Avenue, just on the lip of the neighborhood I grew up in. The prep chef, a tall boy with red cheeks, got it for him. Jack somebody. A "rapper." (Everybody, it seemed, "rapped.") I still don't know his last name but sometimes after the night shift, they'd turn up at our house in Chinatown; you could hear them riffing and rhyming and "being bad" in the basement. Unimaginably violent, vulgar (not to mention borrowed) lyrics. You've got to start somewhere, I suppose. No point in playing them "I Want to Hold Your Hand."

I didn't think he'd last four days as a dishwasher. *Un plongeur.* Not that he was a quitter or a sissy, but that job—the lowest on the unforgiving restaurant ladder, eight hours of dirty dishes and encrusted pots—I just couldn't imagine him getting out of bed, getting dressed, going on the subway to do that till midnight.

But I was, as you often are with your children, wrong again. You'd think you know them better than anyone else, all those years up and down the stairs, tucking them in, sad, happy, carefree, worried—but you don't. In the end they always have something in their pocket you never imagined.

Six weeks later, I could barely believe it—he got up one afternoon, bounced into the kitchen with the heavy-footed, happy walk of his, and said, "I got a promotion." Jack, it turned out, had quit to cook in another restaurant and he, Jesse, was the new prep chef. Something in me relaxed about him. Hard to say what it was. Simply the knowledge, I guess, that when he had to, he could do even the shittiest job and make a go of it. (Unlike his father.)

———

Winter came down, early darkness smudged the windows. In the middle of the night, I noticed a fine dusting of snow on the roofs; it made the houses look a bit fairy-talcish, like pastries in a store window. If a pedestrian had approached my basement windows after midnight, he might have heard the angry voices of two tall boys, chefs by day, rappers by night, giving voice to the indignities of growing up in the ghetto, shooting heroin, robbing stores, selling guns; daddy a dealer, mommy a crack whore. A perfect portrait of his childhood! (Jack's father was a born-again Christian and conscientious churchgoer.)

From where I stood at the top of the basement stairs (partially eavesdropping), I couldn't help but notice they were starting to sound sort of—I don't know—cool. They had good chemistry, those gangly boys in their loose-fitting clothes. God, I thought, maybe he's got talent.

One clear, chilly night, an aura of excitement issued from the basement. Loud music, strident voices. Corrupted Nostalgia (as they now called themselves) exploded up the stairs in baseball hats, bandannas, floppy pants, sunglasses, and oversize hooded sweatshirts. Two very bad dudes on their way to their first gig.

Could I come along?

Not a chance. Not even *remotely* a chance.

Out they went, somewhere, Jesse's head thrown back like a black man dealing with an L.A. cop.

And very quickly, it seemed, they performed again, and then again and again, in grubby clubs with low ceilings and unenforced smoking regulations.

"What do you think of our lyrics?" Jesse asked one day. "I know you've been listening."

For weeks I'd known this was coming. I closed my eyes (metaphorically) and jumped into the water. "I think they're excellent." (Just water the plant and keep the T. S. Eliot to yourself.)

"Really?" His brown eyes moved over my face, looking for a fault line.

"May I make a suggestion?" I said.

His face darkened with suspicion. Watch your step now. This is the stuff people remember—and write about—fifty years later. I said, "Maybe you should try to write about something a little closer to your own life."

"Like what?"

I pretended to reflect for a moment. (I'd rehearsed this part.) "Something you feel strongly about."

"For example."

"Like, say, um—Rebecca Ng."

"What?"

"Write about Rebecca."

"Dad." This in the tone of voice one reserves for a drunken uncle who wants to take the family car out for a midnight "spin."

"You know what Lawrence Durrell said, Jesse. If you want to get over a woman, turn her into literature."

A few weeks later, I happened by the top of the stairs when he and Jack were discussing where they were going to play that night. An after-midnight show (along with a half-dozen other acts) at a place I went to thirty years ago to look for girls.

I waited until just after eleven-thirty, then I slipped out into the frosty air. Cut across the park (I felt like a thief), through Chinatown (garbage night, cats everywhere), then up the street until I was almost at the door of the club. There were a dozen young men standing out front smoking cigarettes, blasting lungfuls of smoke into the night air, laughing boisterously. And spitting. They were all spitting.

There he was, a head taller than most of his friends. I slid into a seat at a coffee shop across the street where I could keep an eye on things unrecognized. It was Saturday night in Chinatown: electric-green dragons, exploding cats, all-night eateries with that ugly fluorescent lighting. Across the street, the city's miserable milled about in blankets in front of the Scott Mission.

Five minutes went by, then fifteen; one of the boys bent over—he appeared to be talking to someone on the stairs, just inside the club. Then Jack emerged. Such a fresh-faced kid. He looked like a choirboy. All heads turned toward him. Frosty breath. Shivers. Then suddenly the whole bunch of them rushed inside, the last boy flicking his cigarette butt in a long, graceful arc into the traffic.

I waited till the coast was clear and then nipped across the busy street. I went up the stairs cautiously; I could feel the air change; it got warmer, smellier (like puppies and stale beer) with each step. I heard recorded music from a back room. They hadn't gone on yet. Wait out front till they start, then slip in. I got to the top of the stairs and turned the corner; a young man on a pay phone looked up and caught me right between the eyes. It was Jesse.

"I'll call you back," he said into the receiver and hung up. "Dad," he said, as if he were hailing me. He came toward me, smiling, his body blocking the way into the hall. I peeked over his shoulder.

"Is that the place?" I said.

"You can't come in tonight, Dad. Some night, but not tonight."

He turned me around very gently and we started down the stairs.

"I think the Rolling Stones played there," I said, looking hopefully over my shoulder, his strong arm (how powerful he is!) leading me downward, ever downward, until we got to the sidewalk.

"Can't I just stay for one song?" I pleaded.

"I love you, Dad, but tonight's not your night," he said. (Hadn't I heard that last bit in *On the Waterfront*, Brando talking to his brother in the back of the cab?) "Some ot time—I promise," he said.

Slipping quietly into bed twenty minutes later, I heard my wife turn over in the darkness. "You got caught, eh?" she said.

CHAPTER

IT WAS A CHANCE REMARK that Jesse made one night; we were walking home from dinner and lingered for a moment in front of a one-story wonky house where we'd lived when he was still a child with purple hair and a little stick girlfriend down the street.

"Do you ever stop here?" I asked.

"No. I don't really like it since other people started living in it. It always feels a bit invaded."

The house hadn't changed at all—not a right angle to it, a beat-up picket fence out front. "I never knew how small it was. It seemed huge when I was a kid," he said.

We stayed a while longer, talking about his mom and that time he got arrested for spray-painting the wall of the school across the street, and then, warmed by all this, we drifted southward toward home.

That night, still under the spell of our conversation, I nipped into the video store and rented *American Graffiti*

(1973). I didn't tell him what it was—I knew he'd protest or want to look at the CD and then find something about the package he didn't like or that made the movie seem "too old-fashioned." I hadn't seen it in twenty years and worried that its charm and lightness had aged badly. I was mistaken. It's an entrancing film, profound in a way that initially escaped me. (Good movies are more intellectual than I used to think, at least the process by which they come into being.)

American Graffiti isn't just about a bunch of kids on a Saturday night. When a very young Richard Dreyfuss drops in on the local radio station, there's a gorgeous moment when he catches Wolfman Jack doing his gravel-voiced routine. Dreyfuss suddenly understands what the center of the universe *really* is: It's not a place, it's the embodiment of a desire to never miss out on anything—not somewhere you can *go*, in other words, but rather a place you want to *be*. And I loved the speech the hot-rodder gives, about how it used to take a full tank of gas to "do" the town strip but now it's over in five minutes. Without knowing it, he's talking about the end of childhood. The world has shrunk while you were looking the other way. (Like the wonky house had for Jesse.)

I didn't want to wear out my welcome by talking about Proust and *American Graffiti*, but how else can you look at that beautiful girl in the Thunderbird who keeps appearing and disappearing at the edge of Dreyfuss's vision, except as an example of the Proustian contemplation that possession and desire are mutually exclusive, that for the girl to be *the* girl, she must always be pulling away?

"Do you think that's true, Dad, that you can't have a woman and want her at the same time?" Jesse said.

"No, I don't. But I used to when I was your age. I could never take anyone seriously for long if they liked me too much."

"What changed?"

"My capacity for gratitude, for one," I said.

He contemplated the empty television screen gloomily. "Rebecca Ng is like the girl in the Thunderbird, isn't she?"

"Yeah, but you have to remember that it cuts both ways. It's like your old girlfriend Claire Brinkman, the one on the skates. How do you think she saw *you* after you broke up?"

"Like a *guy* in a Thunderbird?"

"Probably."

"But doesn't that imply, Dad, that if I hadn't broken up with her, she wouldn't have liked me so much?"

"It implies that your unavailability may have made her like you a lot more than she might have normally."

Another thoughtful pause. "I don't think Rebecca Ng cares whether I'm available or not."

"Let's hope not," I said, and turned our attention to other things.

———

I asked David Cronenberg one time if he had any "guilty pleasures" at the movies—things he knew were trash but loved anyway. I set the framework for his reply by admitting a weakness for *Pretty Woman* (1990) with Julia Roberts. It doesn't have a believable moment in it, but it's a disarmingly effective piece of storytelling, one pleasant scene spilling into the next, and very hard to turn away from once it has you in its idiot grasp.

"Christian television," Cronenberg answered without hesitation. There was something about a puffy-faced southern evangelist working a crowd that mesmerized him.

Fearing that the film club was getting a little starchy (we'd done five nouvelle-vague films in a row), I drew up a list of guilty pleasures for our first week in February. I also wanted to steer Jesse away from the vulgarity of not being able to have a good time at a cheesy movie. You have to learn to give yourself over to these things.

We started with *Rocky III* (1982). I pointed out the cheap but irresistible excitement of the sweating Mr. T doing sit-ups and pull-ups in his foul little crawlspace. No mushroom carpets and faggy lattes for him! Followed by Gene Hackman's 1975 film noir *Night Moves*, which features an eighteen-year-old Melanie Griffith as a lecherous nymphet. Watching her from a distance, her "older" boyfriend says to Hackman, "There ought to be a law." To which the deadpan Hackman replies, "There is."

Then on to *La Femme Nikita* (1990). A ridiculous movie about a beautiful junkie turned government hit man. Yet there's something about this film—it has a certain epsilon-minus appeal, probably because it's so terrific to look at. Luc Besson was a hotshot young French director who seemed to understand in his blood cells where to put the camera, who went for the bang-bang of a visual experience and did it with such verve that you forgave him the dumbness and implausibility of the story.

Watch how the film begins—three guys coming up the street, dragging one of their pals. It's like a rock-video, lysergic-acid hallucination of Gary Cooper's *High Noon*. And talk about a shoot-'em-up: Watch the gunfight in the drugstore—you can practically feel the wind from the bullets yourself.

But *La Femme Nikita* was just a warm-up. Now we were ready for it, the king of guilty pleasures, a real piece of trash that makes you ashamed for people to see it in your house. Prurient, inept, and ugly-minded, *Showgirls* (1995) is a take-no-prisoners film. It leaves the audience shaking its head with incredulity: What, we ask, could *possibly* come next in this tale of a young girl who leaves home (and what a home!) to make it in Las Vegas as a showgirl. There's lots of skin for those who care but by the end of the film, you don't. You can't.

"*Showgirls*," I said to Jesse, "is something of a cinematic oddity, a guilty pleasure without a single good performance."

When *Showgirls* opened, it was greeted by howls of disbelief and derision from critics and the public alike. It scuppered the career of its star, Elizabeth Berkley, before it even started; veteran actor Kyle MacLachlan (*Blue Velvet*, 1986) disgraced himself with a leering, mustache-twirling performance as the "director of entertainment." Overnight *Showgirls* leaped to the top of everyone's worst-film-of-1995 list. Screenings went interactive, with strangers shouting rude remarks at the screen.

But the ultimate compliment came from New York's gay community, where drag queens put on reenactments of the movie, lip-synching the words while the original masterpiece played out behind them on a giant screen. It was simply the most fun since *Mommie Dearest* (1981).

I asked Jesse to count the number of times Ms. Berkley runs from a room, indignant. I brought his attention to a scene where she pulls a switchblade on a cabdriver. A very special bit of acting.

"Instructive terribleness," Jesse said. His vocabulary was improving.

"*Showgirls*," I concluded, "is a film that makes a proctologist of us all. Some people may insist that *Plan 9 from Outer Space* is the worst film ever made, but that's inherited thinking. This one gets my vote."

Somewhere around the time when Ms. Berkley was licking a steel pole in a strip joint, I realized that I had given *Showgirls* a longer introduction than I had *The 400 Blows* and the whole French New Wave.

We kept the guilty-pleasures momentum going with *Under Siege* (1992), a yummy bit of nonsense that boasted two villains, Gary Busey and Tommy Lee Jones, both superb actors, both gnawing on the material. A pair of real *jambons*. You just *know* that between takes they were on their knees weak with laughter. I asked Jesse to be on the lookout for the scene where Busey, accused of drowning his own shipmates, replies, "They never liked me anyway."

To wrap up, we rented a few early episodes of the television program *The Waltons* (1972–81). I wanted Jesse to hear those monologues that come at the end of each show, the narrator wrapping things up, memoir-style, from an adult perspective. Why are they so effective? I asked him.

"Huh?"

"How do they succeed in making you nostalgic for a life you never had?"

"I don't know what you're talking about, Dad."

———————

It made me nervous, Jesse and three of his pals driving to Montreal for a rap show. I gave him a hundred dollars, told him I loved him, and watched him crash excitedly out the front door. I called out to him as he was crossing the yard, the three boys sitting soberly in somebody's dad's car.

I don't know what I said to him but it brought him back across the frozen yard. I just wanted a delay, fifteen, twenty seconds, so that if he had been on a rail to death, he would miss it— by yards, by seconds—but miss it because of those few moments.

He came home late the following Monday night with a strange tale. He looked terrible, his skin on the verge of erupting. He said, "One of the guys that came with us was a friend of Jack's. A fat black guy. I'd never met him before. I was sitting beside him in the car, and when we got about a hundred miles outside Toronto, his cell phone rang. You know who it was? Rebecca. It was Rebecca Ng. She lives in Montreal now, goes to university there."

"Jesus."

"The black guy starts talking to her, right beside me. I tried to read or look out the window—I didn't know what to do. I couldn't think straight. I thought I was going to have a heart attack or my head was going to explode, just like that guy in the movie . . ."

"Scanners."

"Then he says into the phone, 'Jesse Gilmour is here. Do you want to talk to him?' and he passes me the phone. There she is. I haven't seen her for a year, nothing, but there she is. Rebecca. My Rebecca."

"So what did she say?"

"She's making jokes and flirting and, you know, being Rebecca. She says, 'Wow, this is such a surprise. Like totally unexpected.' So she asks me where I'm going to stay in Montreal. I said a hotel, and she said, 'What are you doing tonight? Not just hanging around the hotel, I hope.'

"And I said, 'I don't know. Depends on the guys.' And she says, 'Well, I'm going to be at this club—why don't you come there?'

"It took about six or seven hours to get to Montreal. Maybe longer—it was snowing. We get there and check into the hotel; it's a beat-up place, like a second-rate Holiday Inn but it's right downtown in the student ghetto."

"So you went out and bought a whole ton of beer—"

"We went out and bought a whole ton of beer and brought it back to the hotel; we were all in the same room, a cot for the black guy who knew Rebecca. Around ten or eleven o'clock that night—"

"All of you pretty lit."

"All of us pretty lit, we head out for the bar. This club Rebecca mentioned. Down on Saint Catherine Street somewhere. Students all over the place. I should have understood what that meant. But I didn't. We go into the place and this great big guy with a mustache cards us. He asks for I.D. Which I don't have. The other guys do. And they all go in. But the guy won't let me past. I even told him my ex-girlfriend was in there, I hadn't seen her for a long time. I said all kinds of stuff. None of it worked. So there I was, stuck on the sidewalk, all my friends inside, Rebecca inside, and I'm thinking this is the cruelest thing that's ever happened to me.

"But then Rebecca comes to the front door. She's looking the best I've ever seen her, just—sickeningly good. She talks to the doorman, you know, Rebecca talk, standing close to him, looking up, batting her eyes. Really laying it on. And the guy, the bouncer, gets this kind of embarrassed smile on his face and, without looking at me or at her, lifts up the cord and lets me go in."

"Wow." (What else can one say?)

He went on. "I sat on a stool at the bar beside Rebecca and drank a lot really fast—"

"Did she drink a lot?"

"No, but she was drinking. It doesn't take much with Rebecca."

"And?"

"And I got really drunk. Really, really drunk. And we got into an argument. We were shouting at each other. The bartender cut me off; then the bouncer came over and told us both to leave. So we're out on the sidewalk, it's stopped snowing now but cold, Montreal cold, you can see your breath, and we were still having this fight. And I asked her if she still loved me. She said, 'I can't have this conversation with you, Jesse. I just can't. I'm living with somebody.' She flags down a cab and gets in."

"Did you see her again?"

"More stuff happened—don't worry." He stopped and stared off across the street as if he had remembered something, like suddenly recognizing somebody right in front of you.

"What?" I said, alarmed, sounding cross.

"Do you think I came off like a wimp asking her that? Asking if she still loved me?"

"No. But you know—" I thought about it for a second, how to phrase it.

"Know *what*?" he asked quickly, as if I had a knife under my jacket.

"It's just what I've been saying for the last year or so. Which is that important conversations are never best conducted when you've been drinking." (Jesus, listen to me, I thought.)

"But that's the only time you really want to have them," he said.

"Yes, that's the problem. Anyway, go on."

He did. "We went back to the hotel, us four guys. Somebody had a bottle of tequila."

"Jesus."

"I woke up in the hotel room the next morning with a terrible hangover. Beer bottles everywhere, still in my clothes, all my money spent. I kept remembering asking Rebecca if she still loved me and her saying, 'I can't have this conversation,' and getting into a cab."

"Terrible."

"Trying to get back to sleep."

"Right."

"I must have planned a million times what I was going to say to her when I ran into her, and then this happens."

He stared at the house across the street. "Have you ever done anything like that?" he asked.

"What happened next?" I said.

"We went out for breakfast. I must have been still drunk because when I got back to the hotel, I threw it all up."

"What did you pay for it with?"

"I borrowed some money from Jack. Don't worry—I'll take care of it."

He paused and lit a cigarette. Blew the smoke away. "I don't remember what we did the next day—went to Mount Royal, I think, but it was too cold. I didn't bring the right jacket and I didn't have any gloves. We hung around there for a while—there was some kind of student rally, we thought it might be a good place to meet girls—but the wind was just whistling around the hill, blowing my pant legs.

"We went to the rap show that night, which was pretty good except I kept looking around for Rebecca. I could *feel* her in the concert hall, I knew she was there, but I couldn't see her. Next morning, the fat black guy said he had to go over to Rebecca's to get something, a package."

"Did you go?"

"I wanted to see her. So why pretend?" (He's more courageous than I am, I thought.)

"We went over to her place. Where she lives with her boyfriend. And when we went up in the elevator, I said to myself, This is the elevator she takes every day; and this is the hall she walks along every day; and this is her door . . ."

"Jesus, Jesse."

"She wasn't there; neither was her boyfriend, just a

roommate, some girl, who let us in. But I went over and took a peek in her bedroom. I couldn't help myself. I thought, That's where she sleeps, that's where she gets dressed in the morning. And then she turns up. Rebecca. Looking like she's spent an hour in front of the mirror, picking her clothes."

"She probably had."

"I sat there in the corner watching her talk to the guys. Being Rebecca. Chatting and joking and talking to everybody but me."

"And then?"

"Then I got up and left and we came home."

"That must have been a long ride."

He nodded absently. He was already back with Rebecca on the freezing street, asking her if she still loved him.

CHAPTER

AND THEN THE SUN CAME OUT. It was right
after a Kurosawa film. It must have been *Ran*. Jesse seemed
more than usually engaged, loved the war scenes, loved the
beheading of the treacherous mistress; the final scene where
the blind Fool stumbles his way to the edge of the cliff left
him dizzy.

Over the past few days Jesse's demeanor had changed. He
had the peculiar keenness of a young man with something to
look forward to. Something rather close at hand. I wondered
if it was the weather, beautiful spring days, yellow days, the
smell of damp earth, the retreating grimness of winter, that
had given him so transparent a lift. I sensed that whatever it
was, it was private; yet at the same time he was dying to talk
about it. A direct question, I knew, would spook him, drive
him underground, so I had to play it passively, wait for the
moment when just a look from me might catch his eye and
pull the story out of him like a hook.

We sat on the porch, the fumes from *Ran* slowly dispersing, the birds chirping, our Chinese neighbor working in her garden, putting in the poles for her vines and mysterious fruits; she was in her late seventies and wore beautiful silk jackets. Overhead the round sun blazed down in this unnatural season.

"The thing about March," I said in as dull a voice as possible, "is that you think winter's over. Doesn't matter how many years you've lived here, you still make the same mistake." I could see Jesse was barely listening so I plodded on. "You say, Well, that's it—we've broken the spine of winter. And no sooner, Jesse, no sooner are those words out of your mouth than you know what happens?"

He didn't answer.

"I'll tell you what happens. It starts to snow. And snow and snow and snow."

"I've got a new girlfriend," he said.

"Spring's a tricky time," I said. (I was boring even myself.)

He said, "You remember that story you told me about Arthur Cramner, your old friend? The guy who took one of your girlfriends?"

I cleared my throat. "Not that it matters, son—it was many years ago—but he didn't exactly take her away. I *gave* her away before I was ready to, that's all."

"I know, I know," he said. (Was he hiding a smile?) "But sort of the same thing has happened to me." He asked if I remembered his friend Morgan.

"Your friend from work."

"The guy in the baseball hat."

"Oh yeah, that one."

"He had this girlfriend, Chloë Stanton-McCabe; they'd been together since high school. He was pretty casual about her. I used to say to him, 'You should be careful about her, Morgan—she's really beautiful.' And he'd go"—here he mimicked a dullard's voice—"'Yeah, whatever.'"

I nodded.

"She goes to university in Kingston. Takes economics."

"And she's with *Morgan*?"

"Morgan's a cool guy," he said quickly (and bewilderingly). "Anyway, about a year ago, they broke up. A few days afterward, Jack, the guy in my band—"

"Another guy in a baseball hat."

"No, that's Morgan."

"I'm joking."

"Jack's the guy with red cheeks."

"I know, I know. Go on."

"Jack phoned me one night and he said he'd met this girl in the bar, Chloë Stanton-McCabe, and she'd gone on and on about me, what a cute guy I was, how funny I was. Just everything."

"Yeah?"

"And the strange thing is, Dad, when I went to bed that night I lay in the dark wondering what it would be like to be with her, to be *married* to her. I hardly knew her. I'd seen her at parties and in a few bars but nothing special and never by herself."

"That must have been a nice phone call to get out of the blue."

"It was. Definitely. But a week later, she and Morgan got

back together. Which was a bit disappointing. But not too. I had other girlfriends. But yeah, it was disappointing. Quite, actually."

He stared across the street; bedsheets, a small child's shorts, hung from an improvised clothesline on the second floor. You could smell the warm breeze coming up the street.

He went on. "And one day Morgan said to me—it was after work, he was a bit drunk—he said, 'My girlfriend had a crush on you for, like, a *week*,' and laughed, like the whole thing was a joke. I laughed too.

"I saw Chloë a few times after that; she was pretty flirty but she was still with Morgan. I'd be standing at the bar and I'd feel a hand on my behind and I'd turn around and I'd see this blond-haired girl walking away from me. I asked Morgan once—I asked him how he'd feel about me asking her out and he said, 'Fine, I don't care. I just like sleeping with her, that's all.' Except that's not the word he used."

"I bet."

"But I was super careful never to come on to her. I didn't want Morgan laughing at me, saying, 'I don't even *want* her and you can't get her.' "

"Nice."

"So." He looked across the street as if to gather himself, to get the footing necessary to do justice to this new installment. "Last weekend I went to a bar down on Queen Street. It was like that scene in *Mean Streets*. I'd just had a shower and washed my hair and I had all new clothes on and I felt really good. And I went into the bar and there was this song playing I really like and I felt like I could just get *anything* I wanted

in the whole world. And there was Chloë; she'd come back
for the weekend. She was sitting at a table with her friends
and they all went, 'Ooooo, Chloë, look who's here!'

"So I went over and kissed her on the cheek and said,
'Hi, Chloë.' I didn't stick around, though. I went to the end
of the bar and had a drink by myself. In a little while she
came over; she said, 'Come outside and have a cigarette
with me.'

"We went outside; we sat on the railing in front of the bar
and I said it, just like that, I said, 'I'd really like to kiss you.'

"And she said, 'Really?'

"I said, 'Yeah.'

"And then she said, 'What about Morgan?'

" 'I'll take care of Morgan,' I said."

"So did he find out?"

"I told him the next day. He said" —Jesse lowering his
voice an octave— " 'Whatever. I don't care.' But that night
we went out for a beer after work and he got really drunk,
really fast, and said, 'You think you're so bad 'cause you're
with Chloë now, don't you?'

"But he called me the next morning; it was sort of sad,
sort of courageous too, and said, 'Look, man, I'm just feeling a bit weird about you being with her.'

"And I said, 'Yeah, me too.' "

He lit a cigarette, holding it on the other side of the chair
from me.

"That's a hell of a story," I said (the laundry stirring in the
soft breeze). He sat back, staring straight ahead, imagining
God knows what, Lamaze classes with Chloë, touring with
Eminem.

"Do you figure that Morgan and I will survive this? I mean our friendship. You and Arthur Cramner survived."

"I have to be honest with you, Jesse. Women can be a kind of a blood sport."

"How so?" he said. He wanted to talk about Chloë Stanton-McCabe some more. The story had been too quick in the telling.

It was a good summer for both of us. I got work here and there (it seemed to be gathering momentum), a few television guest shots, a trip to Halifax for a radio book show, another interview with David Cronenberg, a piece for a men's magazine that got me to Manhattan. I wasn't breaking even, more money was going out than coming in, but I no longer had the feeling that I was hemorrhaging money, that something sad, even tragic, awaited me five years down the road.

And then something happened that felt like the period at the end of a sentence. It made me feel that my bad luck had run its course. To the eyes of an outsider, it was no big deal. I was invited to write a film review for a national newspaper. The pay was low, it was a one-shot gig, but—how to explain this—it was something I had always wanted to do. Sometimes these things have a lure well beyond their actual value, like an academic wanting to give a lecture at the Sorbonne or an actor being in a movie with Marlon Brando. (Maybe it's a terrible movie. Doesn't really matter.)

Jesse was working the evening shift. He was still a prep man, washing and cutting up vegetables, cleaning squid, but sometimes they let him work the grill, which had the same slightly disproportionate lure that my film review did. These things are dismayingly arbitrary.

Grill guys are tough, very macho; they like to sweat and swear and drink and work impossible hours and talk about "pussy" and "welfare bums." Now Jesse was one of them. He liked sitting around in his whites after his shift—it was his favorite time—smoking cigarettes and rehashing the night, how they got slammed just after nine (a load of customers arriving all at once), how they'd put a waitress in the "penalty box" (delayed her orders). You never fool with the boys in the kitchen.

There was a kind of strange, pseudo-gay banter in the kitchen—all kitchens, he said—guys calling each other fags, who takes it up the ass, etc., etc. The one thing you couldn't call someone was an "asshole." That was serious—that was a real insult.

He liked it when Chloë picked him up after work, this Marilyn Monroe with a diamond stud in her nose. All the guys sitting around, noticing.

"Do you like her?" he asked me one night, his face very close to mine.

"Yes," I said.

"You're hesitating."

"No, not at all. I think she's terrific."

"Yeah?"

"Yeah."

A moment's thought. "If she broke up with me, would you say that?"

"I'd take your side."

"What do you mean?"

"That means I'd say whatever I had to say to make you feel better."

Pause. "Do you think she's going to break up with me?"

"Jesse. Jesus."

———————————

We watched movies but not so often now. Maybe two a week, sometimes less. It felt as if the world were pulling us both from the living room, and I had a feeling that something precious was coming to its natural conclusion. *Fin de jeu.* The finish line.

I introduced a Buried Treasures program.

I showed him Robert Redford's *Quiz Show* (1994), which gets better, richer, every time you see it. It's the story of a handsome, charming university professor, Charles Van Doren (Ralph Fiennes), who gets caught up in the game-show scandals of the fifties, where contestants, it turned out, were given the answers ahead of time. Like the fixing of the World Series in 1919, it was a stab in the heart of a naïve but trusting American public. That one of their golden boys—and the son of a preeminent scholar, Mark Van Doren (played by the great Paul Scofield), should be in on it made the wound that much more painful.

Like *The Great Gatsby*, *Quiz Show* takes you into a morally slippery world but makes it so beautiful you understand why people go there in the first place and why they choose to stay there. I directed Jesse's attention to the terrific chemistry between Rob Morrow, who plays the congressional investigator, and Ralph Fiennes, who says yes, once, to something he should say no to.

Some of the best acting in the film, the most powerful moments, comes here from Ralph Fiennes's eyes. (For some scenes, it seems as if he might even be wearing some extra eye makeup.) I suggested to Jesse that he wait for an exchange when someone asks Fiennes how "Honest Abe Lincoln" would do on a television game show. Watch what Fiennes does with his eyes. Watch how they move about when he's talking to Rob Morrow: There's a kind of peekaboo quality; he keeps looking at the young man as if he's saying softly to himself, How much does he know? How much does he know?

There's a sequence when they're playing poker: Fiennes makes his bet and Morrow says, "I know you're lying." You can almost hear Fiennes's heart beating when he responds with almost breathless paranoia, "Bluffing. The word is bluffing." He reminds you of Raskolnikov in Dostoevsky's *Crime and Punishment.*

"Do you ever miss being on television?" Jesse asked when the movie was over.

"Sometimes," I said. I explained that I missed the money, but what I really missed was having a dozen utterly superficial, thirty-second conversations with people I hardly knew. "That can put a little sparkle in your day," I said, "believe it or not."

"But do you actually miss being *on television?*"

"No. I never miss that. Do you?"

"Do I miss having a dad who's on TV? No, I don't. I never even think about it."

And with that he got up and wandered upstairs, his physical carriage, the casualness of his movements—for the moment anyway—no longer that of a teenager.

———————————

More Buried Treasures. Like eating banana-cream pie right out of the fridge. (Never mind getting a plate.) *The Last Detail* (1973). "Here are five reasons," I said, "why we love Jack Nicholson."

1. Because, in his words, "It's not hard to make it to the top. What's hard is staying there." Jack's been making movies for forty-five years. Nobody can be "just lucky" or fake it that long. You've got to be great.
2. I love that Jack Nicholson plays a detective—for a significant part of *Chinatown* (1974)—with a bandage on his nose.
3. I love that moment in *The Shining* when Jack catches his wife reading the demented pages of his novel and asks her: "How do you like it?"
4. I love the fact that Jack waited until he was fifty before taking up golf.
5. I love it when Jack slaps his gun on the bar in *The Last Detail* and says, "I *am* the motherfucking shore patrol!"

Some think Nicholson's finest performance, ever, is in *The Last Detail*. He plays "Bad Ass" Buddusky, a cigar-smoking, obscenity-spewing navy lifer—a very excitable guy—who pulls a gig escorting a kid across the country to jail. Jack wants to show him a good time, get him drunk and get him laid before his sentence begins.

When the film came out, Roger Ebert wrote that Nicholson "creates a character so complete and so complex that we stop thinking about the movie and just watch to see what he'll do next." Some movies bring swearing to an art form. Remember the gunnery sergeant in *Full Metal Jacket* (1987)? Like eggs, the f-word can be made into a lot of variations and you hear a lot of them in *The Last Detail*. Studio executives wanted to cool down the script before it got in front of the cameras. They were horrified by the sheer number of expletives and they knew, correctly, that Jack Nicholson was going to spit them out with a wicked spin. Recalls one Columbia executive: "In the first seven minutes, there were three hundred and forty-two 'fuck's. At Columbia, we couldn't have that kind of language, we couldn't have sex."

Robert Towne (*Chinatown*), who wrote the screenplay, said, "If you made love for Columbia Pictures, it had to be at three hundred yards distance. But movies were opening up and this was an opportunity to write navy guys like they really talked. The head of the studio sat me down and said, 'Bob, wouldn't *twenty* "motherfucker"'s be more effective than *forty* "motherfucker"'s?' I said no, this is the way people talk when they're powerless to act. They bitch." Towne dug his heels in. Nicholson backed him up—and since Jack was the biggest star around, that was the end of that.

Picking movies for people is a risky business. In a way it's as revealing as writing someone a letter. It shows how you think, it shows what moves you, sometimes it can even show how you think the world sees *you*. So when you breathlessly recommend a film to a friend, when you say, "Oh, this is a scream—you're going to really love it," it's a nauseating experience when the friend sees you the following day and says with a wrinkled brow, "You thought that was *funny*?"

I remember once recommending *Ishtar* to a woman I quite fancied only to have her shoot me that look the next time I saw her. Oh, it said, *that's* what you're like.

So over the years I've learned to keep my mouth shut in video stores, where sometimes I crave to call out warnings to complete strangers, where I want to snatch the movie out of their hands and assure their startled faces that this other movie, the one over here, is a better choice. I have, however, a few standbys, movies I've recommended that have never, ever come back to bite me. *The Late Show* (1977) is one of them. I picked it next.

It's a simple thriller about a broken-down private detective (Art Carney) and a daffy young psychic (Lily Tomlin) who get caught up in a string of murders in Los Angeles. Even though the film is thirty years old, practically no one seems to have seen it. But when they do, at least the people I've pushed toward it, they all respond with a kind of delighted surprise and gratitude. In some cases, I think it's even led people to reevaluate what they thought of me personally.

When I was preparing *The Late Show* for Jesse, I came across Pauline Kael's original review in *The New Yorker*. She loved it but couldn't quite place it. "[I]t isn't a thriller, exactly," she wrote. "It's a one-of-a-kind movie—a love-hate poem to sleaziness."

The Friends of Eddie Coyle came and went very quickly back in 1973. You still can't find it in video stores, not even in the little specialty stores where they stock horror movies from Finland. It was directed by Peter Yates (*Bullitt*), but the real reason to see it is for that sleepy-eyed wizard Robert Mitchum, who plays the small-time crook Eddie Coyle. We all know somebody like Eddie, a guy born to make the wrong decision. Uncle Vanya as a repeat offender.

As time goes by, Robert Mitchum seems to get better and better—that barrel chest, the deep voice, his way of drifting through a movie with the effortlessness of a cat wandering into a dinner party. He had so much talent, and yet, weirdly, it gave him some kind of bullying pleasure to deny it. "Listen. I got three expressions," he used to say, "looking left, looking right, and looking straight ahead." Charles Laughton, who directed him in *Night of the Hunter* (1955), said all that gruff "Baby, I don't care" stuff was an act. Robert Mitchum, he said, was literate, gracious, kind, a man who spoke beautifully and would have made the best Macbeth of any actor living. Mitchum put it another way: "The only difference between me and my fellow actors is that I've spent more time in jail."

As we watched these films, though, I sometimes had the feeling that Jesse's presence was somehow more dutiful than before. Thirty minutes into Woody Allen's *Stardust Memories* (1980), I could tell by his physical posture, the telltale leaning on his elbow, that the film bored him, and I began to suspect that he was watching it for my sake, to keep me company.

"Guess who the cinematographer on *Stardust* was," I said.

"Who?" he said.

"The Prince of Darkness."

"Gordon Willis?"

"Same guy who shot *The Godfather.*"

"Same guy who shot *Klute*," he said absently.

After a diplomatic pause, I said gently, "I don't think he shot *Klute.*"

"Same guy."

I said, "I'll bet you five bucks that Gordon Willis did *not* shoot *Klute.*"

He was a graceful winner, no gloating, when he lifted his bum off the couch to slip the money into his back pocket, his eyes not meeting mine. "I always thought Michael Ballhaus shot *Klute*," I said milkily.

"I can see that," he said. "Maybe you're thinking of those early Fassbinder flicks. They're kind of grainy."

I stared at him until he looked up. "What?" he said. Knowing perfectly well "what."

CHAPTER 13

FALL 2005. CHINATOWN. Chloë, having changed
her major to business administration, went back to school
in Kingston, Ontario. Shortly thereafter Jesse announced he
wanted to quit his restaurant job and go up north to write
music for a month with a friend of his, a guitar player I
barely knew. The guy's father was an entertainment lawyer
and had a big house on Lake Couchiching. A boat too. They
could stay there rent free. Get jobs as dishwashers in a local
restaurant. What did I think? It wasn't really a question—we
both knew that. I said sure.

And then, like that, he was gone. I thought, Well, he's
nineteen—that's the way it goes. At least he knows that Michael Curtiz shot two endings for *Casablanca* in case the sad
one didn't work out. That's bound to help him out there in
the world. Can't ever be said now that I sent forth my son
defenseless.

For the first time, the blue room on the third floor in Chinatown was empty. It was as if someone had sucked all the life out of the house. But then, by around the second week, I started to like it. No mess in the kitchen, no sticky finger stains on the fridge handle, nobody crashing up the stairs at three in the morning.

Occasionally he phoned home, mildly dutiful calls: The trees were bare, the lake was cold, but the job was fine; everything else was pretty good. They were writing lots of songs. Lying in the boat at night, wrapped in a blanket, staring at the stars, his friend strumming a guitar. Maybe he and Joel (that was the guitar player's name) were going to get an apartment when they got back to town. Chloë was coming up one of these weekends.

Then one day (people on bicycles with gloves again), the phone rang and I heard Jesse's voice. Shaky, like a man who can't find himself in the present, like ice sliding out from under your feet.

"I just got canned," he said.

"From your job?"

"No. Chloë. She just canned me."

They'd been bickering on the phone (his directionless life, his loser friends; "waiters and airport personnel," she called them). Somebody crashed the phone down on somebody. Usually she called back. (This had happened before.) But not this time.

A few days passed. On the third morning, a bright, copper-leafed day in the country, he woke up certain, as certain as if he had seen it in a movie, that she'd found another boyfriend.

"So I called her cell phone," he said. "She didn't answer. It was eight o'clock in the morning." Not a good development, I thought, but said nothing.

He phoned her during the day from the restaurant kitchen; left several messages. Please call. Will pay long-distance charges. All the while this conviction, this *certainty* growing like an ink stain throughout his body that something very serious was happening, that he was standing on ground he had never stood on before.

Finally near ten o'clock that night, she called him back. He could hear noise in the background. Music, muffled voices. Where was she? In a bar.

"She called you back from a bar?" I said.

He asked her if there was anything wrong; he could barely find his voice. Like talking to a stranger. "We have some things to talk about," she said. Indistinguishable words. It sounded, he wasn't sure, as if she'd put her hand over the mouthpiece and ordered a martini from the bartender.

He didn't waste time (he's always impressed me that way), and went straight to it. He said, "Are you breaking up with me?"

"Yes," she said.

Then he made a mistake. He hung up on her. Hung up and waited for her to call back in tears. He paced back and forth in the living room of this cottage up north, staring at the phone. Talking out loud to her. But no ring. He called her back. He said, "What's going on here?"

Then she did her part. She'd been thinking about it, she said. They weren't right for each other; she was young, she was going to college, she was on the cusp of "an exciting future in the workforce." One cliché after another, all delivered in this new, girl-on-the-go voice; he'd heard traces of it before, but now it didn't make him want to strangle her—it made him frightened of her.

He said, "You're going to regret this, Chloë."

"Maybe," she said breezily.

He said, "That's it then—I am out of your life."

"And you know what she said then, Dad? She said, 'Bye-bye, Jesse.' She said my name, real softly. It just broke my heart hearing her say my name like that, 'Bye-bye, Jesse.' "

His friend Joel came in later that night after his shift in the kitchen. Jesse told him the story.

"Really?" Joel said. He listened for about ten minutes, threading new strings onto his acoustic guitar, and then, or so it seemed, lost interest and wanted to talk about something else.

"Did you get any sleep?" I asked.

"Yes," he said, sounding surprised by the question. I could tell he wanted something from me but at the same time knew there was nothing I could give him, except a direction in which to blow the poison that had been collecting in his body over the past few days.

Finally I said (uselessly), "I wish I could help you."

Then he started to talk. I can't remember what he said, it's not important, it was just talk and talk and talk.

"Maybe you should come home," I said.

"I don't know."

I said, "Can I give you some advice?"

"Sure."

"Don't go on a drug or drinking binge. Have a few beers.

I know you feel terrible, but if you go on a binge, you're going to wake up in the morning and you'll think you're in hell."

"I already do."

"Trust me," I said. "It can get a whole lot worse."

"I hope you still love me."

"Of course I do."

Pause. "Do you think she's got a new boyfriend?"

"I have no idea, honey. I don't think so, though."

"How come?"

"How come what?"

"How come you think she doesn't have a new boyfriend?"

"It'd just be rather fast, that's all."

"She's awfully pretty, though. Guys hit on her all the time."

"That's not the same thing as her going home with them." I regretted the choice of words as soon as I said them. They opened the curtain on a fresh screen of images. But he had already moved on to the next thought.

"You know what I'm afraid of?" he said.

"Yes, I do."

"No," he said, "*really* afraid of."

"What?"

"I'm afraid she's going to sleep with Morgan."

"I don't think that's going to happen," I said.

"Why not?"

"It sounds like she's finished with him."

"It wouldn't bother me so much if it was someone else."

I didn't say anything.

"But I'd feel really terrible if it was Morgan."

There was a long pause. I could see him in that country house, the lake deserted, the trees bare, a crow cawing in the forest.

"Maybe you should come home."

Another long, thoughtful pause in which I could feel him imagining horrible things. He said, "Can we talk a little longer?"

"Sure," I said. "I got all day."

————————

Sometimes when the phone rang late at night, I hesitated for a second. I wondered if I was up to it, to be in the presence of his unfixable agony. Sometimes I thought, I won't answer. I'll do it tomorrow. But then I remembered Paula Moors and those scary winter mornings when I woke up too early, the whole terrible day yawning in my face.

"Do you remember saying that Chloë bored you sometimes?" I said to him one night on the phone.

"Did I say that?"

"You said you were afraid to travel with her because she might bore you on the plane. You told me you used to hold the phone away from your ear because you couldn't listen to her careerist prattle any longer."

"I can't remember ever feeling like that."

"You did. That was the truth of it."

Long pause. "Do you think it's childish that I'm talking to my father about this? I can't talk to my friends. They say stupid things—they don't mean to, but I'm afraid they're going to say something that's really going to hurt me. You know what I mean?"

"I surely do."

A slight change of tone, like a man finally confessing to a crime. "I called her," he said.

"And?"

"I asked her."

"That was courageous of you."

"She said no."

"No to what?"

"No, she wasn't sleeping with anyone but it was none of my business if she did."

I said, "That's a shitty thing to say."

"*None of my business*? A few days ago we were together and now it's none of my business."

"What did you—?" I stopped myself. "What does she *think* you did to make her so mad?"

"Morgan treated her like shit. Cheated on her all over the place."

"Really?"

"Yeah."

"But what did *you* do, Jesse?"

"Do you think I'm ever going to get a girlfriend as good-looking as her again?"

On it went. I had other concerns in my life that fall: my wife, a big magazine piece on Flaubert, tiles falling from the roof, another film review for "that newspaper," a tenant in the basement who couldn't pay her rent on time, a molar that required a crown (Tina's insurance covering only half), but there was something about Jesse's sexual horror I could not put out of my mind.

People said, "He'll be fine. That's life; it happens to us all," but I *knew* those movies you run in your head in the middle of the night—I knew they can make you almost insane with pain.

And it was odd too that just when I was getting used to him being gone, to him having been pulled out into the world by the force of advancing life itself, now, in a way, I had him back. And I didn't want it this way. I would have been much happier to be the guy at the bottom of the social list, the father you have dinner with when all your friends are busy.

CHAPTER 14

H E CAME HOME A FEW WEEKS LATER, a cold time when the wind blew up and then down our street like a mugger; it waited for you to go outdoors and then when you were too far from home, it grabbed you by the collar and gave you a smack. I remember those first days very clearly: Jesse in a wicker chair outside staring off into space, moving the same threadbare furniture around inside his head, trying to find a pattern to make it less awful, a way out of the unacceptable now.

I sat out there with him. The sky cement-gray as if it were an extension of the street, as if the two met somewhere way off on the horizon. I told him every horror story that had ever happened to me: Daphne in grade eight (first girl who ever made me cry), Barbara in high school (dumped me on a Ferris wheel), Raissa in university ("I loved you, baby, I really did!")—a half-dozen stabbings at close range.

I told him these stories with relish and zeal, the point being I had survived them all. Survived them to the point that it was fun to talk about them, the horror of them, the "hopelessness of the moment."

I told him these stories because—and this I tried to hammer into his bean—I wanted him to understand that not one of these dollies with an ice pick, these girls and women who had made me weep and writhe like a worm under a noonday magnifying glass was *someone I should still be with.* "They were right, Jesse. In the end, they were right to leave me. I wasn't the right guy for them."

"Do you think Chloë was right to leave me, Dad?"

Mistake. I hadn't counted on the car turning into that driveway.

Sometimes he listened like a man under water breathing through a reed, as if his very survival counted on hearing the story, the oxygen it gave him. Other times—and I had to be careful—it could spark terrible fantasies.

It was like he had a piece of broken glass in his foot; he couldn't think about anything else. "I'm sorry to keep talking about this," he'd say and then talk about it some more.

What I didn't tell him was that in all probability it was going to get worse, much worse, before it got better, before he landed in that ice cream zone of the present, when you wake up thinking, Hmm, I think I have a blister on my heel. Let me see now. Why yes! I do. What a paradise to find yourself in! Who ever would have believed it?

I had to be careful with the movies I picked. But even then, even when I picked something that had nothing to do with sex or betrayal (not many of those around, I'm afraid), I could see that he was using the screen as a sort of trampoline for his agonizing fantasies, that by resting his eyes in that direction, he could fool me into thinking he was engaged, while in truth, he was moving around the inside of his head like a burglar in a mansion. Sometimes I heard him groan with pain from what he'd found.

"Everything okay over there?" I'd say.

He'd shift his tall body on the couch. "I'm fine." I gave him another smash of Buried Treasures, like giving a kid his dessert before the main course. Anything to get his attention off his own excoriating imagination. Anything to make him laugh.

I showed him *Ishtar*. I've taken hit after hit for this film but I remain obdurate. No one would disagree that the story stumbles when the two failed musicians, Warren Beatty and Dustin Hoffman, arrive in the desert kingdom of Ishtar and get embroiled in local politics. But before and after, there are such comic gems, Warren and Dustin wearing little headbands and singing their hearts out and doing a two-step. Heaven. *Ishtar* is a fine, flawed film that was garroted at birth because a peevish press got tired of Warren having so many pretty girlfriends.

It didn't help Jesse, though. I might as well have shown him a documentary on a nail factory.

We watched a lot of Buried Treasures over the next few weeks. I could feel Jesse's agitation on the couch beside me; it felt as if his body were coiled, like an animal waiting in the dark. Sometimes I'd stop the film. I'd say, "Do you want to keep going?"

"Sure," he'd say, coming out of a trance.

There's a story about Elmore Leonard I've always liked. During the fifties, he was an advertising copywriter for Chevrolet. To come up with a jazzy buzz line for their line of half-ton trucks, Leonard went into the field to interview the guys who drove them. One guy said, "You can't wear the son-of-a-bitch out. You just get sick of looking at it and buy another one."

The Chevy executives laughed when Leonard presented it to them, but said no thanks; that wasn't quite what they had in mind for the nation's billboards. But it was exactly the kind of talk that turned up in Leonard's novels a decade later when he turned to crime fiction. It captured the feel of ordinariness without actually being ordinary.

Do you remember this scene from the 1990 Elmore Leonard novel *Get Shorty*? Chili Palmer gets an expensive coat ripped off in a restaurant; he doesn't say, "Hey, where's my coat—it cost four hundred bucks." No, no. Instead, he takes the owner aside and says, "You see a black leather jacket, fingertip length, has lapels like a suit coat? You don't, you owe me three seventy-nine." That's vintage Elmore Leonard dialogue. Amusing and *specific*.

Or how about this little bit of business from his 1995 thriller *Riding the Rap*. U.S. Marshal Raylan Givens has just come upon two unsuspecting felons in the middle of a carjacking. Leonard describes what follows this way: "Raylan put the shotgun on the two guys . . . and did something every lawman knew guaranteed attention and respect. He racked the pump on the shotgun, back and forward, and that hard metallic sound, better than blowing a whistle, brought the two guys around to see they were out of business."

There have been lots of films based on Elmore Leonard novels. *Hombre* back in 1967 with Paul Newman, *Mr. Majestyk* (1974), *Stick* with Burt Reynolds in 1985, *52 Pick-Up* (1986). More often than not, these early films didn't appreciate the black humor and the outrageously good chit-chat that characterized Leonard's novels. It took a generation of new and younger filmmakers to get those things right. Quentin Tarantino made a lovely, if slightly too long, film called *Jackie Brown* (1997); *Get Shorty* nailed the Elmore Leonard tone; it's also worth noting en passant that it was the film's star, John Travolta, who insisted that the dialogue from the novel be used in the film.

And then in 1998 came director Steven Soderbergh's *Out of Sight* with George Clooney and Jennifer Lopez. Critics loved it but people didn't buy tickets and, same old sad story, it dropped out of sight very quickly. Which was too bad because it was one of the best films of that year. It's a classic Buried Treasure, and that's why I picked it for Jesse.

Before we rolled I asked him to watch for an actor named Steve Zahn in the film. He plays a kind of stoned-out loser named Glenn. I don't know if he actually steals the movie from Jennifer Lopez and George Clooney but he comes awfully close. Here's an unknown actor, a Harvard graduate, by the way, who couldn't even get an audition for the film, who had to make his own audition video and send it to the director. Soderbergh watched fifteen seconds of the tape and said, "Here's our guy."

Again, I don't know how much of the film Jesse actually

saw. He seemed to come in and out of the story, and I think he was relieved when it was over; he skedaddled upstairs pretty fast.

Then I hit it, a movie that was so good, that knocked Jesse so hard on his behind, for a few hours he appeared to stop thinking about Chloë entirely.

Years ago, walking down Yonge Street in Toronto on a summer's day, I ran into an old friend. We hadn't seen each other for a while and decided to see a movie on the spot, the best way to go to the movies. We looked in at a nearby theater, six films playing. "You got to see this one," he said. "You just have to."

So we did. *True Romance* (1993) is an almost unbearably watchable film. A treat you should let yourself see only twice a year. Quentin Tarantino wrote the screenplay about cocaine, murder, and puppy love when he was twenty-five years old. It was his first screenplay. For five years he shopped it around—no takers. It had a kind of freshness that studio heads confused with "doing it wrong." It was only when he made *Reservoir Dogs* (1992), when the "word" was out on him, that the British director Tony Scott took it on.

True Romance has an eight- or nine-minute encounter between Dennis Hopper and Christopher Walken that may well be, for me, the best stand-alone scene in film. (I know you get to say that only once and I've saved it up.) It is exhilarating to watch what good actors can do when the "architecture" of beautiful dialogue is under their feet. You can feel also their pleasure in each other's work. They're showing off. As I sat in the dark theater, as the scene began,

Christopher Walken announcing, "I am the Antichrist," my friend leaned over and whispered, "Here we go."

There are other considerable treats in the movie: a theatrical Gary Oldman as a dreadlocked drug dealer; here's a man who's so completely at home with violence that he can, as Jesse observed, "eat Chinese food with chopsticks seconds before it happens." There's Brad Pitt as a California pothead, Val Kilmer as the ghost of Elvis Presley— it just goes on and on.

I told Jesse to hang on for the film's final declaration of love, Christian Slater and Patricia Arquette frolicking on a Mexican beach, the sun setting in a blaze of gold and bloodred clouds, her voice saying, "You're so cool, you're so cool, you're so cool."

It made him feel good, that last scene. Gave him some kind of private goose, as if there was some beautiful girl out there who was going to catch *him* gliding down a bar some night when just the right song was playing. "You are *so* cool."

Later, we were huddled in coats on the porch, the first snow falling in glittering sparkles that vanished when they hit the ground. "I never liked watching films with Chloë," Jesse said. "I hated the things she said."

"You can't be with a woman you can't go to the movies with," I said (sounding like Grandpa Walton). "What sort of things did she say?"

He watched the snow falling for a moment; in the light from the street lamps his eyes seemed very shiny, like glass. "Stupid things. She was trying to be provocative. It was part of her young-professional thing."

"That sounds rather tiresome."

"It is when you're watching a film you really love. You don't want somebody trying to be 'interesting.' You want them just to love it. You know what she said once? She said Stanley Kubrick's *Lolita* was better than Adrian Lyne's." He shook his head and hunched forward. For a second he looked like a young soldier. "That's got to be wrong," he said. "Adrian Lyne's *Lolita* is a masterpiece."

"It is."

He said, "I showed her *The Godfather*. But just before we started I said, 'I don't really want to hear any criticisms of this film, okay?' "

"What did she say?"

"She said I was being 'controlling.' That she had a right to her opinion."

"What did you say?"

" 'Not about *The Godfather* you don't.' "

"What happened then?"

"We had a fight, I imagine," he said wearily. (All thoughts lead to Rome.) The snow seemed to fall harder now; it spun and twirled by the streetlights; you could see it against the headlights of the cars as they moved down our street. "I just wanted her to love it. That simple."

"I don't know, Jesse—this doesn't sound like a dream love affair to me. You can't go to the movies together because she bugs you; you can't go for a walk with her because she bores you."

He shook his head. "Funny," he said after a moment, "I can't remember any of that stuff now. I can only remember having a great time."

My wife came out; the porch light went on. There was a shriek of chair legs on the wood. The conversation halted, then started up again. She knew not to leave. After a while I left the two of them alone. I thought there was something she could tell him that might make him feel better. She had been quite the party girl, our Tina, in her university years. I knew there was a spin she could put on this Morgan business but I had a feeling I should absent myself for the anecdote it would entail. At one point I looked out the living room window; they were sitting very close together. She was talking, he was listening, then, to my surprise I heard something I didn't expect; the sound of laughter—they were laughing.

It became something of a ritual at the end of the day for the two of them to retreat to the porch for a cigarette and a chat. I never accompanied them; it was private and it comforted me to know Jesse had an older woman (breathtakingly experienced) to talk to. I knew she told him things I probably didn't know about her "party years," as she called them. I never inquired what was exchanged between the two of them. Some doors are best left shut.

I see from my yellow cards that I contemplated showing him *It's a Wonderful Life* again, but, afraid he'd see Chloë in the Donna Reed role, I pulled back at the last second and showed him *Murmur of the Heart* (1971). I was reluctant to play a French art film—I knew he wanted to be entertained—but here was a film so good I thought it was worth a shot.

Like *The 400 Blows*, Louis Malle's *Murmur of the Heart* is about growing up, about the strange awkwardness, the extravagantly rich interior life that young boys experience at the very beginning of manhood. It is a period of remarkable

vulnerability that writers love to return to—I suppose because it's a time when things register profoundly, when the
cement is still soft.

The boy in *Murmur of the Heart* seems to carry that vulnerability in his body, the slightly rounded shoulders, the gangly arms, the sort of giraffelike bumping and banging as he
makes his way through the world. There is a feel of terrific
nostalgia about this film, as if the writer, Louis Malle, was
writing about a time in his life when he was very, very happy
and didn't realize it till years later. It is also a film that savors
the small details of adolescence with such a keen eye that it all
feels familiar—there are flashes of recognition, as if you, too,
grew up in a French family, in a small town in the fifties.

And what a climax. It's hard to believe that anyone could
end a film the way Louis Malle chose to end this one. I won't
say any more except to add that every so often an event happens in your life that reminds you that no matter how well
you think you know someone, even though you think you
can account for every important moment of his life, you
don't and you can't.

"Good *God*!" Jesse said, looking over at me first with incredulity, then with uncomfortable amusement, then admiration. "Now there's a director with balls!"

While we were watching these Buried Treasures, Jesse
making observations here and there, it again surprised me
how much he'd learned about movies over the past three
years. Not that it mattered that much to him; he would have
traded it all, I think, for the phone to ring.

"You know," I said when the movie was over, "you've become quite an accomplished film critic."

"Yeah?" he said absently.

"You know more about movies than I did when I was the national film critic for the CBC."

"Yeah?" Not much interest. (Why do we never want to do the things we're good at?)

"You could *be* a film critic," I said.

"I just know the stuff I like. Nothing else."

After a bit, I said gently, "Indulge me here, okay?"

"All right."

I said, "Off the top of your head, can you tell me three innovations that came with the French New Wave?"

He sort of blinked and sat up. "Um, low budgets—?"

"Yep."

"Fluid camera work—?"

"Yes."

"Movies going outside the studios and into the streets?"

"Can you name three New Wave directors?" I said.

"Truffaut, Godard, and Eric Rohmer." (He was getting into it now.)

"What is the expression in French for New Wave?"

"Nouvelle vague."

"What is your favorite scene from Hitchcock's *The Birds*?"

"The scene where you see an empty jungle gym over Tippi Hedren's shoulder and the next time you see it it's full of birds."

"Why is that good?"

"Because it lets the audience know something bad is going to happen."

"And what's that called?"

"Suspense," he said. "Like Hitchcock building a second staircase in *Notorious*." He rimed it off, the blasé certainty pleasing him. For an instant I had a feeling he was daydreaming that Chloë was hearing all this, a third person in the room.

"Who was Bergman's favorite cinematographer?"

"That's easy. Sven Nykvist."

"What Woody Allen film did Nykvist shoot?"

"Actually, he shot two. *Crimes and Misdemeanors* and *Another Woman*."

"What did Howard Hawks say constituted a good film?"

"Three good scenes and no bad ones."

"In *Citizen Kane*, a man describes something he saw on a dock in New Jersey fifty years before. What was it?"

"A woman with a parasol."

"Last question. Get it right and you get another free dinner out. Name three directors from the New Hollywood movement."

He extended an index finger. "Francis Coppola"—pause—"Martin Scorsese"—longer pause—"Brian De Palma."

After a moment I said, "See what I mean?"

It must have put a little fizz in the air because later that night he slipped a CD-ROM into my computer. "It's rough," he said by way of an introduction. It was a song he'd written up north on one of those nights when the wind sucked at the windowpanes, when Chloë was gone and never coming back.

It started with a violin playing the same petite phrase over and over, then the beat came in, bass and drums, then his voice.

Most of us, I know, think our kids are wizards even when they're not (we stick their smudgy little paintings up on the fridge like Picassos), but this song, "Angels"—I listened to it just the other day, long after all this nonsense about Chloë had come and gone—I can say this: There was something remarkable in this message to a faithless young woman. You could hear a confidence of delivery that seemed to come from someone *other* than the boy presently sharing a couch with me, his lips mouthing the lyrics.

But that wasn't what struck me most forcefully. The big change was in the lyrics. They excoriated one moment, implored the next. They were harsh, meant to wound, obscene, as if the writer had turned himself inside out like a cucumber fish. But they were also, for the first time, *true;* no more bullshit about growing up in the ghetto or corporate greed or threading his way through the needles and the condoms in his childhood backyard. "Angels" was the real deal—as if someone had torn off a layer of his skin and recorded the howl.

Listening to the song, I realized—with relief, oddly enough, not discomfort—that he had more talent than I did. Natural talent. It was the agony over Chloë that had uncovered it. She had burned the baby fat from his writing.

As the voice on the CD faded, as the plangent violin faded (it was like a saw going back and forth, a wound being prodded and probed), he said, "What do you think?"

Slowly, thoughtfully, so he could savor it, I said, "I think you've got talent to burn."

He leaped to his feet exactly as he had done that time I asked him if he wanted to quit school. "It's not bad, is it?" he said excitedly. I thought, Ah, this may be the way out of Chloë.

———————

I came home late that evening. The porch was dark; I didn't see him at first until I was almost on top of him. "Jesus," I said. "You scared me." Behind him through the kitchen window I could see Tina moving around in the brightly lit kitchen and I went in to her.

Normally, Jesse, hungry for conversation, would have followed me into the house, yakking about this and that. Sometimes he'd even plant himself outside the toilet, talking through the door. I exchanged the day's pleasant news with my wife (here a job, there a job, everywhere a job, job) and drifted back outside. I turned on the light. Jesse craned his neck around to see me, a tight smile drawn on his lips.

I sat myself quietly beside him. "You know that thing I was afraid of happening?" he said.

"Yes."

"It happened."

A friend had called, given him the news over the phone.

"Are you sure?"

"Yep."

"How do you know it's Morgan?"

"Because he told my friend."

"Who then told you?"

"Yes."

"Jesus, why would he do that?"

"Because he still likes her."

"I mean why would your friend tell *you*?"

"Because he's a friend of mine."

The Chinese woman across the street came out with a broom and began vigorously sweeping her steps. I barely dared look over at him.

"I think she's making a terrible mistake," I said impotently.

Sweep, sweep, went the broom, the woman jerking her small head around like a bird.

"I'll never take her back now," he said. "Never."

He slid off the chair and started down the porch steps, and as he did I noticed his ears. They were red, as if he had been sitting forward in his chair and rubbing them. There was something about his red ears and the way he walked away —as if there were nowhere to go, as if all tasks, all human action, except *her*, were futile, an empty parking lot extending all the way to the horizon—that clutched at my heart and made me want to call out after him.

———————

I was just about to show him a Jean-Pierre Melville film, *Un Flic* (1947), but he wanted to watch *Chungking Express* instead. He fetched it from his room upstairs. "Do you mind?" he said. "I want to watch something from *before* Chloë." But halfway through the film, "California Dreamin' " soaring off the screen, the reed-thin girl twirling and dancing in the apartment, he took it off. "It's not working," he said. "I thought it might inspire me."

"How would it do that?"

"You know—I got over Rebecca; now I'll get over Chloë."

"Yes?"

"But I can't get back there. I can't remember what it was like to *like* Rebecca. It only makes me think about Chloë. It's too romantic. It's making my hands sweat."

He didn't come home the next night, leaving instead a rather tense, rather solemn message on the answering service to the effect that he was staying the night at the "studio." I'd never seen this place, but I knew it was small, "not enough room to swing a cat." Which meant where exactly would Jesse be sleeping? And then there was the tone of voice, its inappropriate gravitas. The voice of a young man confessing to stealing a car.

I slept uneasily that night. Near eight in the morning, still bugged, I called Jesse's cell phone and left a message, said I hoped he was well, could he call his father when he got a chance. And then, apropos of nothing, I added that I knew he was feeling terrible, but that drugs of any kind, cocaine in particular, would probably land him in the hospital. Maybe kill him.

"There's no ducking this one," I said, pacing back and forth in my empty living room, the sun speckling the porch outside. "There are no shortcuts." I sounded pompous and utterly unconvincing. But when I put the phone down, I felt calmer; tweedish as I'd come across, at least I'd said it.

Twenty minutes later, he called back. Odd for him to be

up so early. Still, there he was, sounding a little deep-chested, a little careful, as if someone were holding a gun on him or watching him very closely as he spoke to me.

"Is everything okay?" I said.

"Yes, yes, it really is."

"You don't sound so good."

This provoked a peevish snort. "I'm going through something pretty unpleasant here."

"I know you are, Jesse," I said. Pause. He didn't jump in. "So we'll see you tonight."

"We might be rehearsing," he said.

"Yes, well, I'd like to see you afterward. Have a glass of wine with Tina."

"I'll do what I can," he said.

Do what I can. (I'm not asking for a voluntary deposit at the blood bank here, sonny.)

I had a very strong feeling not to push him, that he was far, far out on a leash and that the leash had grown mysteriously thin. Eminently snappable. I said good-bye.

It was a strangely beautiful day, blindingly sunny, the trees bare, the clouds marching briskly across the sky. An unreal day.

The phone rang again. Dull voice. Bereft of inflection. "I'm sorry I lied to you," he said. Pause. "I *did* take drugs last night. I'm in the hospital now. I thought I was having a heart attack; my left hand went numb, so I called an ambulance."

"For fuck's sake," was all I could manage.

"I'm sorry, Dad."

"Where are you?"

He named the hospital.

"And where the hell's that?"

I heard him cover the phone. He came back on and gave me the address.

"Are you in the waiting room now?" I said.

"No. I'm here with the nurses. In bed."

"Stay where you are."

Moments later, while I was dressing, his mother called. She was rehearsing a play down the street; could she come over for lunch?

I picked Maggie up in Tina's car and we drove through that bright afternoon to the hospital, parked the car, walked three miles through hallways, talked to someone at the emergency reception desk; doors slid open; past a knot of joking nurses and everyday doctors and blue-uniformed paramedics, turned left, then right, to bed number 24. There he was. Whiter than death. His eyes like marbles, his lips blackened and crusted, his fingernails filthy. A heart monitor beeped over his head.

His mother kissed him tenderly on the forehead. I stared down at him coldly. I looked at the heart monitor. I said, "What did the doctors say?" I couldn't touch him.

"They said my heart was going really fast but that it wasn't a heart attack."

"They said it wasn't a heart attack?"

"They don't think so."

"They don't think so or they *know* so?"

His mother shot me a reproachful look. I put my hand on his leg. I said, "That was good you called an ambulance." I almost said (but stopped myself), I hope I don't have to pay for it.

Then he started to cry; he looked up at the white ceiling over his head, the tears streaming down his cheeks. "She won," he said.

"Who?"

"Chloë. She won. She's out with her old boyfriend having a great time and I'm here in the fucking hospital. She won."

I felt my heart being pulled as if by a pair of strong fingers. I thought I might faint. I sat down. "Life is very long, Jesse. You don't know who's going to win this round."

"How did this happen?" he sobbed. "How did this *happen?*"

I could feel my chest starting to shake. I thought, God, please don't make him cry anymore.

"She called up this guy and she fucked him," he said, looking at me with such pain I had to look away.

I said, "I know things look a little desolate."

"They *do*," he cried. "They look so desolate. I can't stand to go to sleep or to close my eyes. I can't get any of these pictures out of my head."

I thought, He's going to die of this.

I said, "Much of the way things look is because of the cocaine, honey. It strips away all your defenses. It makes these things seem even worse than they are." Such useless words, such contemptibly, loathsomely ineffective words. Like flower petals in the path of a bulldozer.

"Really?" he said and the curious tone, like a man reaching for a life jacket, pushed me forward. I talked for fifteen minutes; his mother's eyes never left his face; I talked and talked and talked, anything I could say; I felt as if I were feeling around in a dark room, my fingers seeking here and there, in this pocket, in that drawer, under this piece of cloth, over there by that lamp, looking by touch for the right combination of words that might respark that "Really?" and the momentary relief that came with it.

I said, "You can get over this girl, but you can't get over her with cocaine."

"I know," he said.

They'd just arrived at the studio to rehearse, he began. All day long he'd had a feeling that Jack knew something, that he was keeping it from him. Maybe Chloë had been cheating on him all along, maybe Morgan was the world's best . . . whatever.

So he said, "Do you know something you're not telling me?"

And Jack, whose girlfriend vaguely knew Chloë, said no. Jesse pushed him a little harder. No, there was nothing new, just what he'd already told him five times: that she'd called up Morgan, he'd gotten on a bus and gone to London, they'd spent the evening in the apartment listening to some "really cool" music. And then she fucked him. That was the story, honest, that was all he knew.

And then somebody brought the cocaine out. And then it was seven hours later, everybody asleep, Jesse on his knees looking through the carpet threads for any coke that might have fallen off the table. Then his arm went to sleep; he went outside into the dazzling sunshine, the sunlight gleaming off the cars, and found a bar that was open, said he needed to call an ambulance; the bartender said, "We don't do that here."

So he went to a phone booth—it was nearly noon now, everything rushing by, very frightening, and called 911. Sat down on the curb and waited, the ambulance arrived, they put him in the back. He looked out the back window as they drove him to the hospital; he could see the sunny streets falling away behind him; a nurse asked him what he'd taken, asked him for his parents' phone number; he said no.

"And then I just gave up," he said. "I gave up and told them everything."

For a moment no one said anything; we just sat there looking at our pale son, his hand over his face.

"It was the one thing I asked her not to do," he said. "The one thing. Why did she do that one thing?" You could see it playing out on his pale, childlike features: *She does this to him, he does that to her.*

"A shitty thing to do," I said.

The doctor came in, a young Italian guy, goatee and mustache, very solid. I said to Jesse, "Can you be candid with the doctor if we're here?"

"That's important," the doctor said as if someone had just made a clever joke, "being candid."

Jesse said yes. The doctor asked some questions, listened to his heart and his back. "Your body doesn't like the coke," he said with a smile. "Doesn't seem to like the cigarettes either." He straightened up.

"You haven't had a heart attack," he said. He explained something I couldn't follow, making a fist with his hand to show a heart stopping. "But let me tell you this. Whenever anyone your age *does* come here with a heart attack, it's always because of coke. Always."

Then the doctor left. Three hours later we left too; I dropped his mother off at the subway and took Jesse back to my house. Just as we pulled into the driveway, he broke into sobs again. "I miss that girl so much," he said. "So much."

Then I started crying too. I said, "I'd do anything to help you, anything."

We sat there, both of us sobbing.

CHAPTER 15

ND THEN A MIRACLE OCCURRED (but not a surprise). Chloë, the upwardly spiraling careerist, appeared to be having second thoughts. Morgan, rumor had it, had been dispatched. Feelers were put out. Her best friend "ran into" Jesse at a party, told him that Chloë "really, really" missed him.

The color, it seemed to me, returned to his features; there was even a difference in the way he walked, a bounce that he was unsuccessful in hiding. He played me another song, then another; Corrupted Nostalgia appeared to be, as they say in show business, on a hot streak. They performed in a bar down on Queen Street. I remained exiled.

Sensing that his interest was cooling for our Buried Treasures program, I looked further afield. Something to do with writing, since he seemed to be leaning in that direction now. But there it was, as obvious as the proverbial nose on my face: We'd do a program of movies that were inordinately well written. We'd do Woody Allen's *Manhattan* (1979). Take a look at *Pulp Fiction* (1994), making clear, though, the distinction between fun writing and true writing. *Pulp Fiction*, immensely entertaining as it is, spiffy and glittery as the dialogue is, doesn't have a real human moment in it. I reminded myself to tell him that story about Chekhov watching Ibsen's play *A Doll's House* in a Moscow theater, during the course of which he turned to a friend and whispered, "But listen, Ibsen is no playwright . . . Ibsen just doesn't know life. In life it simply isn't like that."

So why not show him Louis Malle's *Vanya on 42nd Street?* He was too young for Chekhov—it might bore him, yes—but my guess was that he'd love Wally Shawn's whining, complaining, romantically smitten Vanya, particularly when he's ranting about Professor Serybryakov. "We can't all be speaking and writing and spewing forth work like some farm machine!"

Yes, Jesse would like Vanya. "Excellent weather for suicide."

Then for a sort of dessert, I'd show him *To Have and Have Not* (1944). What credentials: based on the novel by Hemingway (loony by then, swilling martinis and popping pills and writing nonsense at four o'clock in the morning); screenplay by the Lolita-loving William Faulkner; with that great Bogart/Bacall scene upstairs in the seacoast hotel where she offers herself to him with this speech: "You don't have to do anything or say anything; or maybe just whistle. You know how to whistle, don't you, Steve? You just put your lips together and blow." Show-off writing of the best kind.

Speaking of which, show him David Mamet's (now there's

a show-off) *Glengarry Glen Ross* (1992). An office of third-rate real estate salesmen, losers to a man, take a verbal whipping at the hands of a "motivator." "Put that coffee *down*," Alec Baldwin says to a stunned Jack Lemmon. "Coffee's for closers only."

This was what I planned. And then maybe we'd do some more film noir, *Pickup on South Street* (1953) . . . It was all ahead of us.

Then came the Christmas holidays: nighttime, Jesse and me outside, snow lightly falling. Searchlights bouncing around the winter sky looking for God knows what, celebrating God knows what. He hadn't seen or talked to Chloë Stanton-McCabe, no phone calls, no e-mail, but she was due to return any day now to spend a week with her parents. There was going to be a party. He would see her there.

"What if she does it again?" he asked.

"Meaning?"

"Goes off with another guy."

I had by this point learned not to make wild, trust-me-on-this-one predictions (I certainly never saw Morgan coming).

"You know what Tolstoy says?" I said.

"No."

"He says that a woman can never wound you the same way twice."

A car drove the wrong way up our one-way street; we both watched it. "Do you think that's true?" he said.

I gave it serious consideration. (He remembers everything. Be careful what you promise.) I did a speed-tour through my personal list of departed lovers (surprisingly long). It was

true, yes, that no woman had wounded me as much the second time she left as the first. But what I also realized was
that for the most part, if not entirely, I had never had the
chance to be wounded twice by the same woman. When my
unhappy lovers headed for the hills, they tended to stay away
for good.

"Yes," I said after a bit. "I think it is."

A few nights later, Christmas only a few days away now,
I was tinkering with the tree, the lights flashing off and on,
some working, some not, an unsolvable puzzle of physics
only my wife could fix, when I heard the customary crashing down the stairs. A smell of vigorous deodorant (applied
with a bicycle pump) filtered into the room, and the young
prince set off into the cold air to discover his fate.

He didn't come home that night; there was a masculine,
adult-sounding message on the service the next morning; a
floor of fresh snow lay on the lawn, the sun already working
its way in the sky. Sometime later that afternoon he returned,
the details of his evening mercifully brief but telling. He had
indeed gone to the party, had made his entrance late with a
number of the lads, a phalanx of baseball hats and oversize
T-shirts and hooded sweatshirts; and there she was, in the
smoke-crowded living room, the music deafening. They had
spoken for only moments when she whispered, "If you keep
looking at me like that, I'm going to have to kiss you." (My
God, where do they learn this stuff? Are they all at home
reading Tolstoy before these parties?)

After that he was vague (which is how it should be). They
had stayed at the party; suddenly there was no hurry, not for
either of them; odd but true, as if the last few months had

been vaguely unreal, had never really happened. (But they did and there would be plenty to be said about *that* later.) For now, though, it was like gently coasting down a hill on a brakeless bicycle; you couldn't stop the momentum even if you tried.

When I think about the film club, I can see now that that was the night when it started to end. It set in motion a fresh chapter in Jesse's life. I wouldn't have thought so at the time; at the time, it looked like business as usual, as if, Well, now that's out of the way, we can get back to the film club. Uh-uh.

Yet even in writing these words, I'm cautious. I remember my last interview with David Cronenberg, during which I made the rather lugubrious observation that raising children was a series of good-byes, one after the other, to diapers and then snowsuits and then finally to the child himself. "They spend their young lives leaving you," I observed when Cronenberg, who has adult children himself, interrupted. "Yes, but do they ever really leave?"

A few nights later, the unthinkable happened. Jesse invited me to watch him perform. He was playing at that club around the corner where the Rolling Stones had once played, where the ex-wife of our prime minister had gone home with one of the guitar players, I believe. The place Jesse had kicked me out of a year earlier. It was, in a word, chock-full of history.

I was told to arrive at the front door a few minutes before one in the morning and to behave myself, by which he meant no awkward demonstrations of affection, nothing that might diminish his aura of danger and heterosexual, hard-bitten "street cred." To which I readily agreed. Tina was not invited; two adoring, misty-eyed adults—that was too much. She also agreed happily. She is a slim woman with little fat on her bones, and the idea of stepping into the freezing air, of possibly waiting in a line for forty-five minutes in the early hours of the morning while icy blasts from Lake Ontario whipped and gusted up the street, relieved her of even the most urgent curiosity.

So at twelve-thirty that night I ventured out onto the icy sidewalk and slipped across the park. I made my way down a deserted street in Chinatown, cats nibbling at unspeakable things in the shadows. Turned the corner, the wind goosing me from behind, until I arrived at the front doors of the El Mocambo. The same group, it seemed, of young men waited there as before, smoking cigarettes, swearing, laughing, gusts of frozen breath hanging like cartoon bubbles just before their faces. And there he was. He hurried over to me.

"You can't come in, Dad," he said. He looked panic-stricken.

"Why not?"

"It doesn't look very good in there."

"Whatever do you mean?" I said.

"There's not that many people; they let the act before us go too long; we lost some of the audience—"

That was enough for me. I said, "You got me out of a warm bed on a freezing night, I got into my clothes and huffed my way over here, it's one o'clock in the morning, I've been looking forward to this for *days,* and now you're telling me I can't come in?"

A few minutes later he led me up the stairs, past the pay

phone where he'd once caught me. (How fast time was passing.) I went into a small, low-ceilinged hall, very dark, with a small square stage at the end. A few skinny girls sat in chairs to the side of the stage. Kicking their legs and smoking cigarettes.

He needn't have worried; over the next ten minutes the doorway darkened with stocky black kids in hairnets and long-framed girls in black eyeliner (they looked like haunted raccoons). And Chloë. Chloë with her diamond nose ring and her big blond hair. (He was right—she did look like a movie star.) She greeted me with the cheerful good manners of a private-school girl encountering her principal in the summer holidays.

I sat in the far corner among giant, black cubes (I never found out what they were, discarded speakers, packing cases—who knows). It was a zone so black I could barely make out the features of the two girls beside me. Although I could smell their perfume and hear their mirthful, obscenity-littered exchanges.

Jesse left me there with the admonition, unspoken, to stay put. He had "some business" to take care of, he said, before he went on.

Sitting in the darkness, my heart thumping with almost unendurable anxiety, I waited. And waited. More kids arrived, the room heated up; finally a young man stepped onto the stage (Was that where Mick Jagger had stood?) and enjoined the audience, amid a barrage of hoots, to get their "fucking shit" together and "give it up" for Corrupted Nostalgia!

Corrupted Nostalgia, no less. And out they came, two

lanky boys, Jesse and Jack; the beat for "Angels" started, Jesse put the microphone to his lips, and out came those lyrics, bitter and demeaning, the howl of Tristan against Iseult; Chloë stood in the middle of the crowd, her head turned slightly to the side, as if to avert the violent onrush of words.

This was no longer just the boy on the couch watching movies. This was "someone else" on the stage in front of me, and I felt it again, a sense of his essential separateness from me, his "ownness" . . .

For Jesse and me, all manner of things lay ahead: A few months down the road, he made a video of "Angels"; Chloë played "the girl" (the actress who'd been hired for the part went on a coke binge and didn't turn up). There were more dinners at Le Paradis, more cigarettes on the porch with Tina (I can hear the conspiratorial rise and fall of their voices even as I write this), more movies, but in theaters now, the two of us sitting on the left-hand side of the aisle, nine or ten rows up, "our spot." There were tiffs with Chloë Stanton-McCabe, brinksmanship and operatic makings-up; there were hangovers and patches of sloppy behavior, a sudden affection for culinary writing, a prickly apprenticeship with a Japanese chef, and a humbling "invasion" of the British music scene ("They have their own rappers over there, Dad!").

There was also a suspicious birthday greeting from, who else, Rebecca Ng, currently in her second year of law school.

Then one day—it seemed to come out of the blue—Jesse said, "I want to go back to school." He signed up for a three-month crash course, math, science, history, all the horrors that had defeated him years before. I didn't think he stood a chance, all those hours and hours and hours of sitting on his bum in a classroom. All that homework. But I was wrong, again.

His mother, the former high school teacher from the prairies, tutored him in her house in Greektown. It didn't all go smoothly, especially the math. Sometimes he rose from the kitchen table shaking with rage and frustration and stormed around the block like a madman. But he always came back.

He started to sleep there—it made things easier in the morning, he explained, "to get right to it." Then he quit coming back to my house altogether.

The night before his final exam he phoned me. "No matter how this turns out," he said, "I want you to know I really tried."

A few weeks later, a white envelope landed in my mailbox; I could barely watch as he climbed the porch stairs, pulled out the letter and opened it, his hands shaking, his head going back and forth as he read down the lines.

"I made it," he shouted, without looking up, "I *made* it!"

He never came back to live at my house. He stayed on at his mother's and then got an apartment with a friend he'd met at school. There was a problem about a girl, I think, but they worked it out. Or they didn't. I can't remember.

We never got around to watching the Great Writing unit. We just ran out of time. It didn't really matter, I suppose; there would always be something we didn't get around to seeing.

He outgrew the film club and, in a certain way, he outgrew me, outgrew being a child to his father. You could feel it coming for years, in stages, but then suddenly, there it was. It can loosen your teeth if you let it.

Some nights I walk by his bedroom on the third floor; I go

in and sit down on the edge of the bed; it seems unreal that he's gone, and for the first few months it haunted me going by there. He's left, I notice, *Chungking Express* in his bedside table; he has no use for it anymore, has gotten what he needed from it and left it behind like a snake its skin.

Sitting on that bed I realize that he will never come back in the same form again. A visitor from now on. But what a strange, miraculous, unexpected gift, those three years in the life of a young man at a time when normally he would begin to shut the door on his parents.

And how lucky I was (although it certainly didn't seem so then) not to have a job, to have had so much empty time on my hands. Days and evenings and afternoons. *Time.*

I still daydream about an Overrated Films unit; how I'm dying to talk about *The Searchers* (1956) and the bewildering praise and nerdy analysis it has spawned; or Gene Kelly's malignant phoniness in *Singin' in the Rain* (1952). We will have time again, Jesse and I, but not *that* kind of time, not that rather bland, sometimes dull time which is the real signature of living with someone, time that you think will go on forever, and then one day, simply doesn't.

Many, many other things lay ahead; his first days in college, his inexpressible delight at a student card with his name and face on it, his first assignment ("The Role of Multiple Narrators in Joseph Conrad's *Heart of Darkness*)," his first after-class beer with a college pal.

But for the moment there was just a tall boy on the stage of an old downtown club, a microphone in his hand, his father hidden in the audience. Sitting there in the darkness with those raccoon-eyed girls in ski jackets, I confess I had a small, private weep. I'm not sure why I was weeping—at him, I suppose, at the *fact* of him, at the unrecapturable nature of time; and all the while those words from *True Romance* repeated themselves over and over in my head, "You're so cool, you're so cool, you're so cool!"

ACKNOWLEDGMENTS

Writing a book about family members, particularly if you adore them, is a harrowing experience and not one I'm likely to reprise anytime soon. To that end my first thanks must go to my son, Jesse, for entrusting me with his portrait and for allowing its publication sight unseen. Thanks also to his mother, Maggie Huculak, for more things than I can enumerate here. I want to also acknowledge the fact that while my daughter, Maggie Gilmour (all grown up now and living in Chicago), does not figure in this particular story, she figures enormously and irreplaceably in my life. I owe her mother, Anne Mackenzie, thanks—and probably money—dating back nearly forty years.

I have dedicated this book to my editor and publisher, Patrick Crean, for salvaging my literary life; thanks also to my agent, Sam Hiyate, for displaying interest and enthusiasm at a time when my phone, apparently, was disconnected. Thanks to Jonathan Karp, Nate Gray, and Cary Goldstein at Twelve; to Marni Jackson for the Tolstoy assignment; and to the boys and girls at Queen Video for their tireless extemporizing about even the most indifferent overnight rental. As always, I must thank the waiters at Le Paradis restaurant, where portions of this book were written.

And of course, without my wife Tina Gladstone's love and insistent reassurance, I don't know what would have become of this book—or of me, for that matter.

FILMOGRAPHY

Absolute Power

Aguirre, the Wrath of God

Alien

American Graffiti

Annie Hall

Another Woman

Apocalypse Now

Around the World in 80 Days

Basic Instinct

Beetlejuice

Bicycle Thief, The

Big Sleep, The

Birds, The

Blue Velvet

Breakfast at Tiffany's

Bullitt

Butch Cassidy and the Sundance Kid

Carlito's Way

Casablanca

Chinatown

Chungking Express

Citizen Kane

Crimes and Misdemeanors

Dead Zone, The

Dirty Harry

Dr. No

Dr. Strangelove

Dolce Vita, La

Domino

Duel

8½

Exorcist, The

Fast Times at Ridgemont High

Femme Nikita, La

52 Pick-Up

Fistful of Dollars, A

Flic, Un

400 Blows, The

French Connection, The

Friends of Eddie Coyle, The

Full Metal Jacket
Get Shorty
Giant
Glengarry Glen Ross
Godfather, The
Godfather Part II, The
Hannah and Her Sisters
Hard Day's Night, A
High Noon
Hombre
Internal Affairs
Ishtar
It's a Wonderful Life
Jackie Brown
Jaws
Jungle Fever
Klute
Last Detail, The
Last Tango in Paris
Late Show, The
Lolita
Magnum Force
Manhattan
Mean Streets
Miami Vice (television series)
Mr. Majestyk

Mommie Dearest
Murmur of the Heart
Night Moves
Night of the Hunter
Night of the Iguana, The
North by Northwest
Notorious
Onibaba
On the Waterfront
Out of Sight
Plan 9 from Outer Space
Plenty
Pickup on South Street
Poltergeist
Pretty Woman
Professional, The
Psycho
Pulp Fiction
Quiz Show
Ran
Reservoir Dogs
RoboCop
Rocky III
Roman Holiday
Rosemary's Baby
Samurai, The
Scanners

Scarface

Searchers, The

Sexy Beast

Shining, The

Shivers

Showgirls

Singin' in the Rain

Some Like It Hot

Stardust Memories

Stepfather, The

Stick

Streetcar Named Desire, A

Swimming with Sharks

Texas Chain Saw Massacre, The

Thief

Third Man, The

To Have and Have Not

Tootsie

True Romance

2001: A Space Odyssey

Under Siege

Unforgiven

Vanya on 42nd Street

Volcano: An Inquiry into the Life and Death of Malcolm
   Lowry

Waltons, The (television series)

Who's Afraid of Virginia Woolf?